# AID TO LIFE

## Montessori
## Beyond the Classroom

Susan Mayclin Stephenson

D1599288

*In a real sense all life is inter-related.*
*All* [humans} *are caught in an inescapable network of*
*mutuality, tied in a single garment of destiny. Whatever*
*affects one directly, affects all indirectly. I can never be what I*
*ought to be until you are what you ought to be, and you can*
*never be what you ought to be until I am what I ought to be...*
*This is the inter-related structure of reality.*

—Martin Luther King, Jr.
*Letter from Birmingham Jail*

## AID TO LIFE,
## *Montessori Beyond the Classroom*

Michael Olaf Montessori Publishing Company
PO Box 1162
Arcata, CA 95518, USA
www.michaelolaf.net
For permission to reprint sections or to translate:
Contact: michaelolafcompany@gmail.com
Author's website: www.susanart.net

ISBN 978-1-879264-29-8

**Front**: After visiting the home of one of the students of the first AMI Montessori 3-6 course in Thailand the author painted this scene. The Buddhist Asoka sustainable community is a model of balanced living, children, adults, including elders, sharing the daily work and fun

# TABLE OF CONTENTS

# GRATITUDE

There are many people who deserve thanks, and credit, for the wisdom in this book.

*My Own Teachers*: First of all, I am grateful to the university philosophy and art professors who helped me begin to figure out what life is about, and the AMI Montessori course lecturers—in London, Denver, Washington DC, and Rome—who gave me the vision, and the skills, to help the world.

*Family*: I am eternally grateful to my husband, who parented and grandparented along with me, and who cheered me on as I walked through every international Montessori project door that opened. And to my children and grandchildren who taught us both so much. I am grateful to our son who chose to homeschool for twelve years—through elementary, middle, and high school—for opening my eyes to the fact that education can be much more than a goal for the future, but a way to flourish here and now, and to make this state of being a life-long habit.

*Students*: Thank you to the students in my Montessori primary classes in the USA, Virgin Islands, and Lima, Peru. There can be no wisdom without the personal experience that comes from many years of interaction with children. I know you taught me at least as much as I taught you.

*Colleagues*: Thank you to the heads of the education departments in several countries, the participants in my workshops, and the audience members at talks. Thank you to the school administrators and teachers who welcomed me to observe and advise them, again, teaching me at least as much as I taught them.

*Readers*: I began writing about Montessori almost half a century ago and am so grateful to those who supported this writing, and to the thousands of readers, and attendees of the workshops and book clubs based on my books, who gave me the feedback, and asked the questions, that required further exploration on my part. And of course all those who recommend and share my books. The thrill of continued learning is one of the most important elements of a Montessori life.

# Introduction

Maria Montessori, MD, was a social activist deeply interested in justice and peace in the world. Her methods were successful in curing childhood traumas incurred by World War I and a major earthquake in Italy to mention just two areas of her work. Because she was also an educator there are many schools today that follow her healing methods and this is very important. But the value of these life-affirming principles has value in many other fields — preparation for birth, aiding elders who are living with dementia, and everyone in between.

The stories in this book begin in a Montessori 6-12 classroom in The Virgin Islands of the Caribbean Sea. It was this foundation, the Montessori classroom teaching experience, which gave me the wisdom and insight to use Montessori principles in a variety of situations.

These experiences include teaching in a girls school in Peru where there were no Montessori materials, answering questions in a newspaper column about the Montessori approach to everyday situations, bringing Montessori help to blind children in Tibet, poor children of the Himalayas in Nepal, and children and young adults with severe disabilities in Russia. You will read about a first-year Montessori project in an orphanage in Morocco, projects shared during an Educateurs san Frontières gathering in Thailand, and a meeting with the Dalai Lama at a conference concerning the educational crisis in the Kingdom of Sikkim. Especially valuable today are two chapters devoted to using Montessori ideas at home, one for parents of children aged 0-6, and the second for parents of children and young adults 6-18.

The book concludes with a brief overview of how Montessori practices differ according to the age and stages of development of children and young adults, an observation of an authentic Montessori 3-6 class, and an enjoyable and inspiring description of a grandchild-grandparent literary week-end (in the child's words), a story which has been shared in Montessori training courses.

When the physical and psychological needs of humans are met, people can come to know more fully who they are. When we are then given the possibility to create and work using our full capabilities, a natural and inborn tendency to take care of the environment, and each other, rises to the surface. Such people can become complete, balanced, productive, valuable and contributing members of society, and happy. This situation can unleash a force that could heal the world.

# PERU, A Montessori Class without Montessori Materials

In the 1970's I was teaching a Montessori elementary class on the Caribbean island of St. Croix. There were fourteen students, from age 6-13, all but three of them completely new to Montessori. A visitor who had graduated from a very well known and respected British-Peruvian girls' school in Lima, Peru was very impressed with what she saw in our elementary class.

For example, early in the year I had become ill and had to stay in bed. My apartment was in the same building as the school and at noon of the first day of my illness a delegation of three students came to petition a change in what was happening in their class. I didn't have an assistant but another staff member had been assigned to take over the class till I returned.

The words of the delegation were, in essence, "She is treating us as irresponsible children. We have our work list and know how to take care of ourselves!"

I thought that was true. They were functioning very independently and responsibly. I met weekly with each student individually to make a list of what was their responsibility to do (bare minimum required by the government), and what they wished to do, during the following week. I held no group meetings or lessons, no scheduled individual lessons. It was up to the students to ask for help or for lessons, from each other or from me — according to their week plan. So I gave them, supported by the administration, permission to be in charge of themselves. It worked; three days later they hardly noticed that I was back in class

The Peruvian visitor wanted very much for these ideas to be available to her alma mater. Always interested in travel, for myself and my two daughters who were in the class, I flew to Lima during spring vacation, applied to teach, and was accepted.

Susan's photo Machu Picchu 2015

In the fall of 1979 we moved to Lima and I took up the new position. At this time there was no Montessori education in Peru, and so no Montessori materials. Upon arrival I was taken to a storage room to see what I could find. There was a base-eight math set, similar to the base ten decimal system materials used in Montessori primary and elementary class, but it was way beyond what we would be doing in this class of girls from the ages 4-6.

However, during my primary and elementary Montessori teacher training we were taught:

Even with a complete set of the highest quality Montessori materials, if the adult is not well trained and suitable to this profession, this will not be authentic Montessori. But when one is well trained and suitable to this profession, it is possible to create authentic Montessori with no materials.

One of the stories we had heard was about a Montessori teacher who was traveling, with her entire family and a large group of adults and children, from one part of Asia to another, migrations caused by the partition of British India into two countries in 1947. Each night as the travel stopped and camp was set up this woman gathered the children and included them, in all of the necessary and important practical life of the group. They had a purpose, value to their community, a way of learning new skills that distracted them from the sadness of their journey. This was authentic Montessori.

"Well," I thought to myself, "if this woman could create Montessori in such dire circumstances, I should be able to do something valuable for the students in a beautiful girls school in one of the world's capital cities."

My job was to teach math and reading and writing in English in the mornings and a Peruvian teacher taught the same subjects in Spanish in the afternoons. The schedule was 1.5 hours first thing in the morning, then a 45 minute break where the girls played outside and the teachers drank tea and ate too many sweets and chatted (and I knitted), then the girls returned for another hour of work before lunch. In a Montessori class there would be at the very minimum an uninterrupted 3-hour work period which goes a long way in helping children to become deeply involved in work and to increase periods of concentration. But this was the schedule so I was required to work with it. I really did enjoy the camaraderie, the tea and cakes, knitting, and sometimes sharing knitting patterns with the other teacher during our breaks.

The materials consisted of the standard workbooks, crayons and paper, a blackboard and chalk, picture books and early readers, my guitar (which I took with me wherever I went), a bell, and whatever cleaning materials I could gather from the janitor.

My assistant became upset when she found out that I was going to teach the girls to sweep, mop, and use powdered cleanser on the furniture. She told me, "When the mothers of the students find out they will remove them from the school because they will ruin their hands and never find a husband!"

There were two directors of this Kindergarten-through-High School institution, one British to ensure British standards, and one Peruvian to ensure Peruvian standards. I immediately went to the Peruvian director to check if what my assistant said was true, and was relieved to have her say, "You go ahead and teach the girls how to clean. They might have to know how to clean a house on their own when they grow up, depending on where they live."

I could see that the children were used to a teacher ringing a bell to get the attention of the group, but I knew from my own teaching experience that adding more noise to existing noise was counterproductive. It was better to whisper and stand still and be calm. This worked well after the girls got used to this.

Then one day, remembering that balanced and happy children exhibit a "love of silence," I taught them what we call in Montessori, the silence game. This game is not a way to impose silence on a noisy group of children, but to learn to be aware of and to create silence. First of all, at a moment when the class was busy and quite calm and quiet, I whispered, "Listen, we are almost making silence." Of course it became even more quiet in the room so I whispered, "Listen, what can we hear?" and together we listened to the sound of the clock ticking and sounds from outside the classroom. The feeling of peace that descended on all of us was palpable.

On another day, during a time like this, I challenged them, just as Dr. Montessori did with her own students, to stand and then sit back down without making a sound, then to continue to sit absolutely still and not move a muscle, and I turned off the light to make the experience again more profound.

One day the head of the kindergarten classes in the school came into the room to talk to me. The girls were being a bit loud at that moment so I turned off the light. Instantly the noise disappeared, the girls stopped moving and sat, immobile and silent, making silence. They looked at the two of us adults with big smiles on their faces obviously proud of this new skill. The director was spellbound.

The news spread. It had already become known that one never heard yelling from our classroom, but our silence game took this to a new level. The director asked if I would help the other kindergarten teachers learn these things. So I began discussing this with the other kindergarten teachers at the morning break time when we all gathered for tea, and then pulled the ideas together and created a paper for the school.

Below is the English version of this paper. Over the years I have shared this many times when working with schools where there were no Montessori teachers and traditional methods of education and classroom management were being used. There have been slight changes but the main ideas remain the same. Here is the paper as it stands today:

# LOWERING THE NOISE LEVEL IN AN OPEN CLASSROOM

by Susan Mayclin
for Colegio San Silvestre, Lima, Peru

*Susan Mayclin wrote this paper in response to a request of mine. I asked her to give a talk to the kindergarten teachers who, naturally, have our biggest noise problem. However, I think we shall all find it most useful to begin with this paper and so I have had it duplicated for you.*

**— "Steve" Eckford, Kindergarten Director,
Colegio San Silvestre**

In order to create a calmer, quieter classroom there need to be changes in the environment, the behavior of the children, and the behavior of the teacher. First observe carefully at different times of the day and perhaps take notes, in order to discover what it is about the children's behavior, the routine, etc., that is causing the noise. Then work on one thing at a time to alleviate the problem.

Once you begin to change a behavior pattern, for example how a teacher handles a specific situation, there are two very important points to keep in mind: All teachers working with a group of the same students should agree to react the same way or the children will be confused. Think a lot about the change before

17

instituting it, and don't regress once you have started a new policy, or the children will not take this or any following change seriously.

Here is an outline of points:

### *Classroom Physical Space and Distances*

What is the Distance Between People Speaking to Each Other? The children should be close enough to the adult who is in charge of them that there is never a need to talk above a soft voice. Calling across the room to each other is probably the practice that causes the most noise and it is the most difficult to change. Whenever I have something to say to my assistant or to a child, I walk over to her and speak quietly, so we are almost the only two people who can hear the conversation.

Aside from this modeling behavior of the teacher, explain the policy of not speaking to each other across the room to the class. I did this first in Spanish through my assistant, and then in English. From then on if I heard a child calling out to me, not walking up to me and speaking quietly, I did one of three things; (1) the first time I go to the child and explain that I would like her to come to me (or raise her hand and I will come to her) and not call across the room. (2) After that, when it happened again (and it did) I asked another child to go and remind the child who is calling out. This reinforces the behavior of both children. (3) Finally, if I knew the child understood the new policy but had forgotten, I ignored her when she called out to me. Then she remembered what to do.

Children at this age (up to 6 or 7 years) still have a "sense of order." Creativity and work is enhanced when the necessary equipment or tools are always kept in the same place. They get used to certain activities taking place in the same physical setting. For this reason it is better not to have loud boisterous activities in the same place where at other times children are expected to sit and work quietly.

All the objects the children use in the course of the day should be accessible to them at any time, and should be able to be reached without making a noise. Are needed items kept in drawers or cupboards that bang? Do cupboard doors slam?

Give fun role-playing lessons, fun games, to show how to carry a chair or tuck in a chair quietly, how to carry scissors, how to carry books and turn pages carefully, how to say please and thank you, or to offer or ask for help.

Do children have to ask, or wait nosily, for pencils, scissors, tape, brooms, etc.? Arrange the room so the children can get these things themselves. Play games to see who can remember where things go, in order to teach them to put things away. And challenge them with the game of putting things away gracefully and "without making a sound." Don't do these games too often or they will become tedious . . . just enough to help the children become aware of the noise they make, and to enjoy the challenge to be graceful and quiet.

## The Class Schedule

The children's "sense of order" extends to the schedule of their time. Children feel secure when they know what is going to happen next. They need confidence of knowing what they will be doing all day, every day, and there should be little variety in the schedule for children at this age. They also need to know that if they begin to become engrossed with a piece of work, focused and concentrating, that they will not be interrupted and asked to stop. Children who are interrupted while concentrating often give up trying to be deeply involved with their work. Respecting and not interrupting deep concentration on purposeful work, chosen by the child, is a hallmark of Montessori practice at any age.

For example, in my class we start every morning with a very short group (fewer than 5 minutes) during which the expected work for the morning is written on the board (i.e. math, number book, patterns, writing letters, story, guitar song, three or four things). The children are then free to do their work for the morning, in any order and anywhere in the classroom. Then when they are finished, they can read, draw, paint or play a few selected games, or help a friend with their work. This was of course one of the major changes and had a lot to do with the girls enjoying school.

Any school-required out-of-the-classroom activities I try to arrange to take place during the last half-hour or hour so the children know that they will never be interrupted until that time.

Observe your class and see what about the schedule could be changed to eliminate a normally long noisy period. Are a lot of children changing activities at the same time? Is there a period when a group of children have nothing to do — but wait noisily? These periods of time are called "transitions" and they can cause boredom and be deadly.

## The Role of the Teacher in Bringing about More Peace and Quiet

It seems to me that children are noisy in class for one of three reasons: they have nothing interesting to do, they are unable to concentrate, or they have not been taught to be quiet. So what can we do to help this situation?

### Support Individual Work

Of course there are the required textbooks, but there must also be something for the children to do when they are finished with this work. They must be free to select puzzles, extra work, quiet games, art, or other age-appropriate materials.

### Observe, then Protect, Concentration

Concentration cannot be taught so we watch out for it and protect it when it occurs. Which children are quiet? When? Why? In my class I know that the children are only quiet during a work period when they are concentrating on what they are doing and that they can only do this when they feel good about themselves and when the work is suited to their interests and abilities. It is very important that this constructive kind of concentration is not interrupted by the teacher or by other children.

I teach this by modeling and by role-playing, first by never interrupting a child if she is concentrating, and second by role-playing "how to watch a friend work without interrupting." The fact that the children in my class have a long uninterrupted work period that is not broken up into short work time blocks helps immensely.

*Teach How to Make Silence and Control Movement*

Just as movement has to be learned (walking, crawling, carrying things, etc.) inhibition of movement has to be learned, and there can be no silence without inhibition of movement.

I have already mentioned lessons of closing a door, cupboard, or drawer quietly. Also we need to teach, as games, walking (instead of running) silently, tucking in chairs quietly, or just sitting quietly. In our class, when the bell rings, for example, which I only do just before the mid-morning break and before the end of the morning, the children arrange their work, fold their hands, close their mouths and sit absolutely still till their table is excused. Then they tuck in their chairs as quietly as possible and silently leave the room. These activities are not commands attained by threats or rewards, but a joyful time that the girls enjoy with smiles of pride on their faces. This is a challenge, and as they do it twice each morning, before break for the required outside exercise for the whole school, the habit subtly lowers the noise level during the rest of the morning, which is an enjoyable and calming experience for all.

*Teach Children How to Help or Teach a Friend*

The children are going to imitate how we teach. One of the best things you can help a child who has finished her work learn to do is to help others. Start with one or two children and casually ask them to help someone who needs help, and to do this in a soft voice. In Montessori classes more teaching is done from child to child than from adult to child. This gives practice in helping others as it strengthens one's own knowledge. And some children will much prefer to learn from another child than from an adult.

### The Attitude and Actions of the Teacher

The attitude and the actions of the teacher are the most important factor. Generally children are not being loud or chaotic because they are bad! So we should not try to make them feel guilty about it. In fact I have known some parents to unconsciously reinforce rude or negative behavior because it was so cute when a child is very young, or because it is the best way to get the parents' attention.

*See Each Child New Each Day*

Always think, "This is a good child." The teacher must see each child new each morning, forgetting misbehavior or transgressions or labeling of the past. Here is a saying that I keep in my mind toward this end:

> *If we treat people as if they were what they ought to be, we help them become what they are capable of becoming.*
> **—Johann Wolfgang von Goethe**

Verbally chastising a child does no good to anyone. It is better to ignore the negative behavior and reinforce the positive. Telling the child in class ahead of time that you are going to ignore, "the way they act when they aren't feeling well when they are not their real self," is respectful, and engages the child in the process of learning self-control.

If you are waiting for a group to get still, notice casually aloud how quickly some have been able to get quiet this time (without a hidden reprimand of those that are still noisy!) In my class, if a child is naughty I remind myself that she is, for some reason that I don't need to discover, not feeling well - and that is why she is not "her usual wonderful self."

I make sure that the children know I feel this way about them. If a child cannot settle down to work, she may be invited to rest in a quiet corner, but only with her agreement "until she feels better," not "until she can behave herself."

### Teach by Teaching, Not by Correcting

This is a main principle of Montessori education. When we see a child doing something disruptive, such as slamming the classroom door, if we correct at that moment, there are a variety of emotions that would come into play, none of them good. So we write down "Give _____ a lesson on closing the door quietly," and we do this at a neutral moment perhaps a few days later.

## Games and Modeling of the Adult

Play games so everyone becomes aware of noise and silence. Together, during a very quiet moment, listen to the noises inside and outside of the classroom, accidently moving a chair, breathing, the ticking of a clock, birds, music or traffic in the street, and, by contrast, "silence."

Don't make more noise yourself. When the noise level goes up, don't add to it by raising your own voice, moving quickly, saying 'shhhh." Instead, step back, pacify yourself, observe what is going on and why and decide what you can do to help the situation. Then act.

When talking to the class as a group, don't let your voice get louder to compete with a rising noise level, but purposely lower it, even to a whisper, to get the attention of the children.

To get the attention of the group for a required announcement for example — teach the children to respond to some signal other than your voice. In our class the signal is to turn the lights off. To teach them, play games to see how quickly they can get quiet on signal (by "quiet" in our class we mean "not moving a muscle"). Don't over practice or overuse this device or it could stop working.

The most important factor in striving for a calmer class is the example set by the teacher. She should move and talk quietly and approach the child to speak to her instead of calling across the room.

## *Conclusion*

Quiet and calm in the classroom should be the result of children engaged in concentration on work they enjoy. Not only will everyone enjoy school more, but also children thrive by learning how to help and teach others, by having their concentration respected, by working at their own speed. Most importantly they will remember what they learn and how they learned.

# EUREKA, CALIFORNIA, A
# Montessori Newspaper Column

After sharing the Peru Montessori experience with a local writer, I was invited to write a Montessori column for *The News*, a newspaper in Eureka, California. Since that time sections of this document have been published as parenting articles by AMIUSA (The Association Montessori of the United States), and have been shared by Montessori schools and teacher training centers.

The column was named *Renaissance Parenting* because it was focused on ways to enable parents and other adults to make use of Montessori philosophy and practice in the everyday life situations. In the 14th century Italy a movement was born named "Renaissance" after the French word for "new birth." The column title represents a new birth in the understanding of Montessori by the general public.

# SELF-ESTEEM IN CHILDREN

*Dear Susan,*

*My question is about self-esteem. Do you think it can be given to a child, or must it come from the child's own achievement? How can we help children who have low self-esteem?*

— Felicia Oldfather, musician

Dear Felicia,

"Self-esteem" is talked about a lot in education and psychology today. It seems to me that there are two kinds of self-esteem being confused as one. One is shallow, transitory, and dependent upon constant or at least periodic validation, reward, or praise from someone other than oneself. It is sort of like the traditional search for "fame, wealth, and power", or grades and the approval of teachers. The other is deep, solid, and dependent solely upon the actions of oneself. The result of the second is more often the self-actualized, content human being who has no need for fame, wealth and power, grades or approval.

The first can indeed be "given" to the child — but it can also be taken away. The second must come from the child's own effort.

We can observe the reason for effort in order to find which kind of self-esteem is being gained. Is the child working or behaving in a certain way in order to get the approval of others or because it is satisfying an inner need?

Even though the word "self-esteem" implies that we are talking about a feeling that comes from the self, very few children or adults in our culture actually get to the highest level of fulfillment, inner peace, and confidence, that comes from loving and being proud of oneself, one's own efforts.

Dr. Montessori's most famous work with children was in the Roman slums of San Lorenzo in 1907. She did not set out to aid children's self-esteem, but that is just what happened. There are many stories about this first Montessori "Casa dei Bambini" (House of Children) which attracted worldwide attention, but one of the main lessons learned is that children, when given the chance, prefer real work to make believe or pretend work. Real work, when not required, rewarded, or manipulated by the adult in any way, and resulting periods of deep concentration, leads to a kind of healing of the spirit. The result is true self-esteem, and an overflowing of love and care for others and for the environment.

In the beginning the first Casa dei Bambini was very much like some modern preschools, beautifully outfitted with dolls, dress-up, make-believe, and adult-led art or other activities. But Dr. Montessori was an astute observer of human nature. She spent many hours taking notes of exactly what the children did during the day, and many hours going over these notes, thinking, and planning changes in the environment to follow the interests of and to attempt to aid the complete development of the children. More and more she saw that the children wanted lessons in an area of work which is today called "practical life" of cleaning and cooking and taking care of oneself and others, and with self-correcting puzzles and other materials which allowed them to refine their senses while completely independent of an adult; activities with what are known as "sensorial materials".

Because the children had shown an interest, and had been allowed to participate in the real work, they ignored the dolls, the dollhouses, the play kitchen, and the other toys. Dr. Montessori showed them different ways to play with the dolls to try and get them interested, but the children could hardly wait to get back to the real work, for this was what fulfilled them and created self-esteem, calmness, and joy. Visitors to the Casa dei Bambini brought the usual gifts of candy; they praised the children for being "good children"; they even sometimes offered the traditional little badges of achievement traditionally given out to reward good behavior.

The children were unaffected, even disdainful, of these rewards. They were not used to working just to please an adult or because of any coercion or reward system. They were working for deeper, more important reasons, and this work fostered the highest level of self-esteem.

Writing about this reminds me of the time I suggested that a young mother visit a Montessori preschool instead of trying to learn about Montessori through books. After her one-hour observation of the class, which began an hour after the children arrived, I asked her what she thought. She replied that it was very beautiful and interesting, "...but", she said, "when do the children get to do what THEY want to do?" I was shocked! I had visited that class many times and I knew that the children were always doing what they wanted to do. I had watched them enter the room in the morning and, with no suggestion from the teacher, pick out the activity each wanted to work on. The choices of the group of children included math work, movable alphabets for writing stories, puzzles for the exploration of size, shape and color, geography puzzle maps, setting the table or washing dishes, painting and then spending a long time scrubbing the easel, and many other activities.

I thought a long time about her question and finally realized that for this mother, as for most of us, working on math, language, cleaning, and geography, were not the favorite choices of our childhood activities. This woman assumed, understandably, that children would rather be playing with dolls or being entertained, than to be concentrating on challenging activities that took effort and concentration.

As adults, what gives us the highest level of self-esteem? Is it watching a movie? Dressing up and being admired for our looks or our clothing? Spending hours weeding and making a garden beautiful? Earning a lot of money? Getting elected president of the board? Earning a degree? Washing windows for money? Washing windows because it feels good? Because it looks nice? Learning a new piano piece, which we thought we would never be able to learn? Winning a piano competition? Which of these gives us the lowest level of self-esteem, the kind that is dependent on praise or recognition from others? Which give us true inner self-esteem? If we discover the difference for ourselves we can better understand the motivation for activity, and the development of true self-esteem in children.

Felicia, as far as the second part of your question, "Can we help children who have low self-esteem?" the answer is: "Certainly we can. But how we go about this depends on the needs and the stages of development of children. I made a comment in the beginning, that very few children or adults in our culture actually get to experience the highest level of self-esteem. I learned a lot about the reasons for this sad situation in a book by Alfie Kohn called *Punished by Rewards, The Trouble with Gold Stars, Incentive Plans, A's, Praise, and Other Bribes*. I'm sure you would find it valuable. Here are some ideas for self-esteem development at different ages.

### Self-esteem in the Newborn

Respecting the natural child-centered rhythms of sleeping and eating, and the development of movement and language, are the keys to helping an infant keep his natural self-esteem. In the womb the child has slept and wakened, and exercised muscles exactly according to physical needs. A child is born with a natural self-esteem; secure that every instinct for sleeping and wakeful movement is correct. Here are some specific ways we can support this natural development of abilities and self-esteem:

1- From the first day on, respect the infant's ability to go to sleep naturally, being careful not to train the infant to become dependent on the actions of someone else for this simple and natural function.

2- Try to never interrupt this natural sleep choice, the sleep-wake rhythm. There is a natural stage of adjustment in the first few days but after that try to follow the child in both sleeping and eating.

3- From the beginning of life do not swaddle the infant, and provide as little clothing as necessary for warmth, so hands and feet are free.

4- Provide movement areas — perhaps a movable mat or carpet — so the infant can spend time with the family while practicing free movement of the whole body.

5- Avoid swings, walkers, and other objects that put the infant into positions he cannot get into independently. Providing free movement on a flat surface gives a message that whatever the infant can do at the moment — turn over, sit-up, crawl, go to sleep — is exactly the right thing.

6- Talk to the infant, as with a child at any age, with the same respectful voice and vocabulary as you would anyone else, not a high-pitched voice and dumbed-down vocabulary or grammar one might use when addressing a pet. The development of language is happening now, by listening and watching.

7- Learn to identify the meanings all of the many vocalizations from birth on. These are real communication that might mean a variety of things such as, "My left arm is asleep," "I want to see my dad," "Someone please talk to me," "This wet diaper feels creepy," "I'm tired of looking at the ceiling," "I am hungry," "Why is everyone in the other room?" "The Mozart sonata is far preferable to that TV ad," "Please touch my head," "Hey, how about a bath!" and so forth.

8- Respond as quickly and as correctly as you can to these requests.

9- Observe to see what the infant is doing before interrupting. The infant may be concentrating on looking carefully at something, learning to move forward on all fours, reaching a rattle, or many other important activities that are important work at this age. If we wait until the infant has completed such an activity before picking him up, the message is that the choice of work is important, and we respect it.

### Self-esteem at Age One

For a year now the young child has watched the family do lots of interesting things, and has been working hard to get up on two legs, with hands freed to join in the real activities of the family. The best thing we can do at this age is to welcome the child, according to the developing abilities, into all of our daily activities. There are hundreds of little ways the very youngest child can join in, in small ways at first, to be part of the daily life.

Here are some specific suggestions:

1- Helping to set the table, even if it is just reaching up and putting the napkins next to the plates

2- Help with brushing the dog

3- Picking dead leaves off of the sidewalk or deck or porch

4- Putting clothes into the washer or dryer

5- Expending the maximum effort in carrying things, climbing, walking long distances. Such challenges and successes build self-esteem.

6- Participating in conversations with adults and older children. Even though the child at this age isn't responding in full sentences, or sometimes even with words, the respect we show a child by listening carefully with full attention and speaking in a normal voice is felt, appreciated, and helpful.

### Self Esteem at Age Two

At this age the child has a strong and healthy need for independence, and encouraging this independence feeds self-esteem. Our skill at this age can mean the difference between "the terrible twos" and "the wonderful twos." Here are a few specific suggestions:

1- Continue with all of the above.

2- Give more choices but only between two alternatives when possible. "Do you want an apple or an orange? "Do you want to use a spoon or a fork?" "Do you want to wear this scarf or that one?" "Do you want me to put your boots on or do you want to do it?" are much more successful than "Eat your lunch. " or "We are going outside now." Giving such choices shows respect and encourages thinking, decision-making, development of movement, and cooperation.

3- Show the child, over and over, patiently, how to put on boots, brush teeth, wipe after using the toilet, clean up spills, put clothes away, brush or comb hair, put on a jacket, all of the activities that, when done for oneself, build self-esteem, improve coordination, and provide for the child's important developing mental and physical independence and responsibility.

4- Communicate with respect. A child knows when he is being ignored in conversation, or spoken down to, in a voice usually reserved for the dog or the cat. We can imagine how it would feel if two people were to discuss us as though we were not even in the room. It is the same for a child. We have all felt the difference in our own self-esteem between being ignored, or included in the conversation.

5 – Phones. Think about how you would feel if you had been having an engaging conversation with a friend, the friend's phone rang and your friend immediately turned away from you, or even walked away from you, to engage in the phone conversation, leaving you alone, ignored, perhaps insulted or hurt. What effect would this have on your own self-esteem? Think about this as you develop the phone policies in the home.

## Self-esteem from Age Three to Six

I haven't mentioned television (or screen time), but, as we can see from all of the activities mentioned above, there is plenty of real and interesting work for children to do when we really get good at including them in our daily lives. Then need for such passive entertainment doesn't even become an issue. Aside from all of the daily work of life, the child is now able to share many of our hobbies and interests, poetry, cooking, gardening, cleaning, washing the car, making music, sweeping the floor, and many things. Here are some specific suggestions:

1- Continue with the above ideas when they are age appropriate.

2- As much as possible do the real work, and engage in pastimes, when the child is at home rather than waiting until the child is out of the house. The child needs to see the work carried out by the older members of the family, and to watch it over and over, in preparation for joining in a bit at a time according to abilities.

3- Model active and joyful actions and facial expressions as you carry out activities that are important in life. (This is helpful for the adult as well as the observing child.) Passive activities done with children such as going shopping or watching TV (or screen time) are far inferior to cleaning, sewing, baking, drawing, building, visiting with friends, offering food to friends, reading, arranging flowers, singing, playing music, all of the most important activities in a happy life.

## Self-esteem from Age Six to Twelve

This is a time for more social interactions, intellectual exploration, and increasing independence. The child changes daily and we have to change to keep up. Analyze your child's day, in school if you are a teacher, at home if a parent. What are you now doing that a child could just as easily do? This is difficult, because we are so used to "taking care of", not realizing that any unnecessary help is actually a hindrance to development. We are so used to doing all of the real life work in the home so our children can concentrate on academics. This robs them of the opportunity to feel really good about being a contributing and valuable member of the family.

I once visited a Montessori 6-12 class where one child welcomed me and got me a chair, another asked if I would like a cup of tea and brought the guest book to be signed. Then I watched two children phone a museum in San Francisco to arrange a field trip and call the parents on the "field trip drivers" list to arrange the transportation. Another child took the attendance and marked off the calendar, and when it was time several children started clearing tables to prepare for lunch, all without a word from the teacher. Imagine the level of self-esteem of these children.

To support the need for independence and responsibility, and to help in developing of a strong self-image, look for tasks that you are doing, that could be done by the child in your school or home.

1- In school, children at this age can help by taking attendance, grading papers, testing each other on math facts, making phone calls, keeping track of state requirements in math, etc., planning the weekly work schedules for themselves, cleaning and organizing the environment, planning and carrying out ecological and social projects, and so on. Look for tasks specific for your own situation.

2- At home, children at this age can help with planning meals, shopping, entertaining and working with siblings (older and younger), cooking and baking, cleaning everything, fixing things that break, organizing shelves and closets, figuring out exactly what the daily family work is and experimenting with different ways to share it, budgeting, making phone calls, writing family thank-you notes, composting, looking for and carrying out service projects, and so forth.

### *Self-esteem from Age Twelve On*

Sometime during these next few years the child quite literally becomes a young adult. It doesn't happen all at once and the development is unique for each person. This stage is very much like that of age 0-3 – a lot of physical growth, emotional ups and downs — sometimes clinging to the family and sometimes wanting to be completely independent. We need to work especially hard to help the young adult find real meaning and purpose in life. And we need to work on ourselves even more because it is very difficult for a parent to realize that baby-infant-child has suddenly all of the needs of an adult!

It is not enough to do school work in the hopes of college success, or for some other future goal. There is an intense feeling, spurred on by the hormones and other physical and emotional and physical changes that something wonderful and important is about to happen. After all for thousands of years this was the age, between 12 and 18, when young people literally took on the role of adults.

There is a need to create and to change things, to break ground with music, clothing, and politics, all of the roles in society. And in the family. It is clear what can happen when this expectation of being the creator of the new fails to be realized. If young adults do not have the opportunity to change by creating in positive ways, they will change in destructive ways.

We can help during this precarious time, and aid the child's self esteem by some of the following methods:

1- Keep communication open, learn and share communication skills.

2- Help with the search for real work and responsibility.

3- Commiserate with the societal and educational demands made on young people today. Listen.

4- Treat the young adult as you would an equal as much as possible, listening to your words and the tone of your voice to see if you would talk to another adult in this way.

5- Be easy on yourself. Realize that there are no blueprints or experts on meeting the needs of adolescents in today's culture.

This is really a pretty brief list, but the thread weaving its way through all of these points is the same: real self-esteem is dependent on what one really thinks about oneself, and it is fed by effort and success on important work. It is participation in activities that call for the coordination of the brain and body working together, concentration, effort, striving for perfection, that call forth the best of the person and build self-esteem.

# WOMB MUSIC

*Dear Susan,*

*When will the best time be to begin teaching our child music? Is there anything we can do while still pregnant?*

— Two string players

Dear String Players,

You are already beginning the music education of your child by playing music during your pregnancy. Many cultures of the past—for example the gypsies of Europe—understood this. It was the best musicians in the group who played for the unborn child. In some cultures the mother or father composes a special song for each child during her pregnancy and sings it daily. When this happens this song is soothing to the child after birth, and creates a special communication between mother and infant.

Many mothers have learned that children in the womb keep time to external music by kicks and other movements, and that a piece of music played often enough before birth will be recognized by the child after birth and can have a calming effect on him. In some Montessori birth preparation classes the parents learn such soothing songs to sing to their unborn child.

Scientists today can trace the specific muscles that are stimulated by specific sounds during pregnancy. High pitches seem to stimulate the upper body of the child, and low pitches the lower body. The implication is that it is beneficial to hear both low and high-pitched voices, and of course a variety of good music. Every spoken language on earth has its own unique set of musical elements such as pitch, rhythm, and timbre. This is known as the *music* of language. It is well known that the music of a language heard before birth improves the child's ability to learn the second language later.

As far as music education after birth, it helps to think about just how a child learns language. For the first days, weeks, months, and years, the child is intensely interested in language, including the music of language. Even the newborn is fascinated with watching mouths as people speak to him. Some think that the reason the length of focus of the eyes in a newborn is exactly the distance of a nursing baby's eyes to the face of the mother is very important. It takes advantage of the many hours a child spends nursing and fosters the physical and psychological bonding; it provides a lot of time for the infant to observe close-up the physical movements of the face during communication. For these reasons it is important that a mother not do anything during nursing that would distract from this important eye contact and the communication, and getting to know each other.

Considering the development of both language and music keep in mind that this is the time the child is taking in and observing (receptive language) in what the child will later express (expressive language). Spoken language, singing, and knowledge of music are not produced in a vacuum, and it does not magically come from nothing at age two or three years. Give your unborn child, and your newborn infant the very best language and the very best music.

As far as music education for the older child, we can also keep in mind the process of learning a language. First the child listens, and gradually, a word or phrase at a time, incorporates more and more language. We do not ask him about his progress in speaking, "Have you practiced speaking for a half of an hour today?" or "Have you said ten 'the's?'" We do not decide what words the child is going to learn each week. We merely fill the environment with language, listen to the child who is trying to express physically or verbally, ignore mistakes, and subtly speak more precisely ourselves. We follow the child's interests, and enjoy the enfolding abilities in spoken language.

The development of music, song, dance, are all as natural as language when approached in this spirit.

Formal music education can begin and be successful at any age as long as it follows the developmental stage of the child, or the adult. I especially like the response Dr. Shinichi Suzuki, of the Suzuki Music Talent Education program, gave to an adult who asked him if it was too late for him to begin to learn to play an instrument his child was studying.     Dr. Suzuki responded, "It is never too late to begin NOW."

# THE MONTESSORI ENVIRONMENT
# BEFORE BIRTH

*Dear Susan, How can we prepare a "Montessori" environment in the home? At what age should we start?*

— Ursula Melvin

Dear Ursula,

Preparation of a Montessori environment in the home begins before birth. Very significant work, in terms of helping parents get back in touch with their best parenting skills, has been done by the Assistants to Infancy Montessori programs, which began in the 1940's in Rome. The adult is the most important "educational material" in the prepared home environment so first of all think about preparing the adult. Today many new parents live far away from family, and have very few models from whom they can learn about parenting. They often have very little real experience themselves of holding and caring for infants. Many young parents get their information from the Internet, from other young parents who are just as clueless. As a result they sometimes have an unrealistic idea that having a baby is a bit like buying a new car or being a good parent is like getting a degree—just put in the time and success will come. When there is not enough preparation, some say that it is during this period, the first months and year of the life of a child, that couples experience the most difficult level of stress sometimes even leading to separation of the couple.

So my advice about the best way to prepare the adult for parenting is to have frequent contact with families and babies, before conception if possible. Read biographies, study "self-actualized" adults and see how they spent their first days, weeks, months of life. Talk to your parents, grandparents, other relatives and friends. Visit day-care centers, schools, and hospital nurseries. Have discussions with your partner about everything you learn. Discuss your beliefs, hopes, and dreams of parenting. Keep a journal. You might have feelings of love, repulsion, joy, doubt, nervousness, and thrilling excitement, as you make your way through this labyrinth of facts, emotions, and impressions. Give yourself permission to put as much time, study, research into this role as you would any other important undertaking in your life. And in the end keep in mind that every parent is doing the best with the information they have.

After putting in the time to learn about the adult, there is much to learn about creating the physical environment for the infant and the constantly changing child. I suggest reading *Understanding the Human Being*, by Dr. Silvana Montanaro, MD, and my own book that has been translated into many languages, *The Joyful Child: Montessori, Global Wisdom for Birth to Three*.

# PACIFIERS AND SWADDLING

*Dear Susan,*

*I see so many young children with pacifiers as a permanent attachment. It doesn't seem healthy. And many are swaddling their infants. As I am gearing up to be a grandmother I am interested in your opinion on this modern phenomenon.*

*— Questioning*

Dear Questioning,

You are right. This is a modern, unhealthy, phenomenon. We live in a very commercial world and new parents are overwhelmed with information, advertisements, and advice on all of the equipment needed for a new baby including pacifiers and swaddling blankets. Both of these might have their place, temporarily or in an emergency, but they should not become permanent. When you think about how many centuries we have done without all this equipment, and in how many areas of the world children grow up happily without these things, it makes it easier to decide what really is necessary.

I have visited homes, yurts or gers, in Mongolia where babies are swaddled and tied by a cord to the wall in order to keep them from falling off of the bed and rolling on to the wood stove because the herding family members were too busy to spend a lot of time watching an infant moving freely. But as soon as the infants begin to crawl they are free to crawl in and out of the yurt, as they like. I have talked to Russian and Eastern European friends who were swaddled as infants because the parents were too occupied during the Soviet Union days to watch the children and give them freedom to move. None of these women went on to swaddle their own children.

The Montessori *Assistants to Infancy*, or birth to three, information for parents (based on the course that began in Italy in 1947) helps families create the best environment in the home for the first three years of life. These families do not use swaddling cloths, cribs, playpens, walkers, swings, bottles, "tippy" cups (cups with lids and a spout that prevent spills but also prevent the child learning about the characteristics of liquids, or developing the careful skill of drinking from a glass), pacifiers, high chairs, or most kinds of baby carriers. All of these relatively new inventions are far more valuable to the manufacturers than to the babies. And we are constantly getting feedback from developmental scientists on why we should not use such unnecessary products in our homes.

For example, as of January 1, 1994, it became against the law to use or keep a baby walker on the premises of any childcare facility, including in-home family day care centers. Gov. Wilson signed the law, known as AB 1858, to ban baby walkers in day care facilities in California. The American Academy of Pediatrics has concluded that baby walkers are dangerous and should not be sold or distributed in the United States. In 1991, 27,800 children under the age of two years were admitted to a hospital emergency room for injuries associated with a baby walker.

According to Consumer Reports magazine, "With a capacity to move as fast as five feet per second, a baby walker can propel your baby faster than you can rescue him."

Yet we are constantly confronted with ads convincing new parents that everyone must have one of these in the home.

Back to the question of pacifiers.

Certainly sometimes a baby needs to have something to suck on or to soothe gums when teething, but these are emergency situations and should be treated as such. A finger, a wooden "teething toy" which needs to be held in the mouth and does not mold to the mouth—and stay there permanently without having to be held there—is best. But there are both physical and psychological reasons not to use pacifiers on a regular basis. You may ask any dentist about the harmful results, to the developing teeth and jaw, of overusing a pacifier.

For a young child two of the most important developmental activities are language and exploring

48

with the mouth. Children put everything in their mouth at that age because the mouth is a capable sense organ — and this is important work. For the two or three years before children develop spoken language, they are using their mouth to practice the physical movements of the mouth, which make up speech. We notice that even newborn children will focus on the mouth of the parent and move their own mouth in response. These vital activities are completely prevented when a child is using a pacifier.

Another reason for not using a pacifier is that a child is forming body awareness at this time and can actually come to think of a pacifier as part of his body! This can lead to a far-reaching oral fixation or self-soothing by keeping something in the mouth at all times - such as cigarettes, food, gum, and so forth.

There is a story I heard a few years ago about a mother and a four-year-old boy who had as company a two-year-old girl and her mother. The mothers and their children visited each other several times a week for quite some time. One day the pacifier fell out of the mouth of the little girl and the boy ran to his mother screaming, "Her mouth fell off!"

My advice to parents is to think about how pacifiers are sometimes used as a quick-fix to solve every discomfort with the oral pleasure of sucking or chewing on a pacifier. It is more important to see what the real need is when a child is crying, bored, loud, whatever situation leads to the use of the pacifier. If the child is bored, offer something to do with the hands, talk or sing together, make it clear that there are many solutions to boredom. If the child is babbling or talking, and you want her to be quiet, take the child some place where she can practice language because this is more natural and healthy than being quiet. Whatever the problem, try to find the correct solution, out of hundreds, instead of solving every problem with a pacifier. I hope you will share this information with the parents of your future grandchildren.

# WEANING

*Dear Susan,*

*I am a homeschooling mom with a new baby and getting interested in Montessori. Is there any Montessori advice for weaning a child? Is it different from La Leche? I found it extremely difficult to wean our 4-year old and I don't want to repeat that scene with our second child.*

— D. R., Centreville, Virginia

Dear D.R.,

*La Leche* (Spanish for "the milk") is an organization that supports breastfeeding instead of bottle-feeding. This organization has done a lot over the years to improve the care of the children, and many Montessori teachers, including myself, are or have been members. But, as in any group of two or more human beings, there are disagreements on many of the individual questions of breastfeeding. What I have found is that everyone recommends what he or she themselves did because they put a lot of effort into being a good mother and don't want to be invalidated. So asking other mothers, or even a La Leche leader, how to breast feed YOUR child is only going to cause confusion.

There are certainly situations, for example in poor areas where there is no clean water to drink, where breastfeeding is important, even for two years or more. Year after year there are regulations by government health organizations on how long an infant should be breastfed. These change. The Montessori system is called "child centered weaning" We watch the developmental signs and then follow the individual child. There is a whole chapter describing this system of weaning in the book, *The Joyful Child: Montessori, Global Wisdom for Birth to Three*.

The advice below refers in these situations. The Montessori Assistants to Infancy program which has been very successful in helping parents with their children for over seventy years is to "follow the child" when deciding how often in a day and for how many months to breast feed, rather than to impose a schedule. They do offer some suggestions that I am happy to share with you:

1- Nurse, or breastfeed, when the child is hungry rather than on a schedule, but aim gradually for a 2 1/2 hour interval so that the child can complete digestion and give his stomach a rest between meals.

2- Completely empty one breast before changing to the second, so that the child can get the nutrients from the end milk, which are different from those of the beginning milk.

3- Introduce new experiences, like tastes of juice, using a spoon, using a glass, during the first year when the child is focusing on the sensorial experience of the mouth, and interested in new experiences of this kind. This does not mean giving the child juice to drink, but just tiny tastes.

4- Avoid pacifiers, bottles if possible, and "tippy" cups, moving directly to a small "shot" glass, and eating utensils. After all, the baby bottle is a relatively recent invention, which came about as an emergency measure.

5—If the mother is the main caretaker, help the father or second adult in the child's life, to find a special daily private ritual to share with the baby, bathing, singing, something just for the two of them, so he does not feel that only the mother is bonding and giving to the child by breastfeeding. During this time the mother should go for a walk and not hover.

6- An important saying in the Montessori world is this: "A good attachment leads to a good separation." This means that if the child's every need, physical, emotional and psychological, is met in the beginning of life, moving on, independently and with confidence, is more likely to be successful.

From the very first day the mother should give her complete attention to the child during nursing instead of talking to another person, reading, talking on the phone, etc. It is no accident of nature that the newborn focus length is exactly as far as the mother's face during nursing. This communication satisfies the psychological and emotional bonding needs. It may be that without this kind of communication while nursing, pacifier dependency evolves, as an attempt to satisfy other than physical needs.

Nursing, or breastfeeding, and weaning are completely natural events. I wish you the best in experiencing these with your second child in a joyful and natural way.

Note: An entire chapter on this subject can now be found in the book *The Joyful Child: Montessori, Global Wisdom for Birth to Three*.

# SUMMER IDEAS FOR UNDER AGE THREE

*Dear Susan, Can you give me some ideas for what to do with a child under the age of three over the summer?*

— a Father

Dear Father,

*Summer.* Does this word bring back memories of long, leisurely days with nothing to do but play with friends and family until the crickets begin to sing and the moon rises? It sounds like the situation in an ancient mythological culture compared to today where both parents work year-round and children have little time off from school, summer camp, television, computers, lessons, and planned activities.

At any age and in any season, special times at home with the family are precious and create the most cherished memories. Especially for the child under the age of three, the best times can be spent at home, working and playing with other family members. Instead of thinking of educational experiences and more toys, think about simplifying the schedule and the environment and enjoying the moment with your child.

One of Dr. Montessori's most well-known sayings is "follow the child," so I suggest jotting down on your planner the activities that appeal to you from the list below; then be ready to offer them to the child to see what works. For some families the best time will be first thing in the morning, for others the afternoon or Saturday morning. Be ready to follow the child in making memories together.

### The First Year

*Sing* – Your child doesn't care if it is the Beatles or Italian Opera, or even if you can carry a tune, as long as it is your voice

*Share your music* – Put on your favorite, be it Bach, Mozart, country-western, Afro-Cuban.

*Dance* – Interpret the music by dancing and enjoy yourself. Dance with your child in your arms, feeling the beat, the interpretation of the mood of the music, and you.

*Talk* – With eye contact and a smile, tell the infant what you are doing, what part of the body is being washed and with what during a bath, during changing and dressing. Talk to your child about what you are thinking, what you remember about your early life, what you hope and dream. There is nothing your child would rather hear than your words.

*Read* – If talking doesn't come easy to you at times, read aloud to your infant the adult book you have been reading silently to yourself. Sometime in the first year the child will begin to enjoy looking at children's books with you as you point and talk about the pictures.

*Explore the home with your child* – As long as it is physically safe, keep the child in the room with you, on a mat on the floor, in the office, the bathroom, the dining room, the kitchen, the porch, the garden. Then your child can fall asleep and wake up following a natural rhythm, and will be happily learning about your family and home.

*Enjoy watching the amazing development of movement in the first year* – Head lifting, reaching, tummy lifting, rocking, crawling, pulling up, cruising along furniture while holding on, walking. Each stage happens only once and you were there!

*Play* – Explore toys with your child. What colors are preferred? What sounds attract attention? Can your child yet grasp a toy? Release it? How many times does your child try? How does it feel to stack blocks or lie next to your infant and watch a mobile stir in the breeze?

*Snuggle* – Nursing may have evolved as a system of providing touch and snuggling many times a day, but as long as the child is not deep in concentration on important work, snuggling is important anytime of the day.

### The Second and Third Years

In the second and third years the child will want to imitate everything you do and participate in the important work of living. It shows great respect and love to encourage this. Keep on singing and dancing, listening and talking; add percussion instruments to your time together, and non-fiction books on many subjects. Your child would rather have real child-size tools to use with the parents than a room full of toys to play with alone. Following are some suggestions for arranging the environment to include the child and examples of things you can do together.

*Kitchen/dining room* – A drawer or shelf with the child's own dishes and flatware, placemats and napkins to set the table, and a small pitcher to fill water glasses one at a time. Also child-size mixing bowls and spoon, broom and mop, bucket and sponge. A child of this age can even cut the stems off flowers, place them in small vases, pour water into the vase, and decorate the table with arranged flowers.

*Living room/family room* – A shelf in the family bookcase for children. Perhaps a couple of CD's for the child to choose for the parent to play. Puzzles, an easel, poster paints with chubby brushes, clay, crayon, and paper can be enjoyed by both of you and eventually the child alone.

*Laundry area* – A child-size laundry basket makes it possible for a very young child to carry laundry with you. This child can put things in the dryer, take them out, and eventually even learn to fold napkins, pillowcases, and washcloths, and put them away in the proper place.

*Bedroom* – A low closet rod and drawers allow the child to help put away clothing and get it out to practice undressing first, and then dressing.

*Outside* – A place to keep small gardening tools, a small wheelbarrow or basket for gathering leaves or weeds, sand and water toys, buckets, a scrub brush to help wash the car, an outside broom to sweep the porch and sidewalk. These all enable the child to work alongside the parents, and eventually independently.

*Fun away from home* – Going out doesn't always mean to the park or swimming pool or shopping. A walk around the block that can take an adult ten minutes can take a child two hours if the adult follows his or her interests. The child at this age can, and wants to, walk long distances instead of riding in a stroller and will delight in discovering the variety of plants and insects, dried leaves, and stones along the way.

*The child's purpose and concentration* – The most important thing to keep in mind is that the child is not doing these things for practical reasons, but out of enjoyment. He or she will repeat what has been chosen over and over, and work at his or her own speed. When we observe repetition and concentration it is time to get out of the way and respect this period of important work. As you play and work with your child, be aware of this important moment when the child begins to concentrate, and take this opportunity to step back and see how long the period of involvement lasts.

Just as we adults become satisfied and refreshed after long periods of concentration, so do our children, from the very early days of life on. In fact this respect for concentration is the most important gift any Montessori school gives any child.

*Siblings* – Where there is more than one child, you will have to put some effort into creating these memories and special times one-on-one with your child at times. It is quite natural for an older child to feel replaced by a younger sibling. Perhaps plan the adult-child time for the three-year-old during the infant's nap, or send just one child to grandparents and keep one with you. Then times with the whole family will be more enjoyable for all.

With these ideas the child will feel wanted, needed, loved, part of the family. We will be providing our time, our energy, our experience, our language, our love, and a wealth of memories that will last a lifetime. Happy summer!

# ADULTS MODELING BEHAVIOR FOR CHILDREN

*Dear Susan,*

*What do you think the most important thing is for parents to model for their children?*

—S.A., McKinleyville

Dear S.A.,

If you don't mind, I would like to answer your question by quoting Dr. Benjamin Spock. At age 92 he has published a book that reflects the wisdom of his accumulated experience, *A Better World for Our Children: Rebuilding American Family Values*. He was asked almost the same question in an interview in an issue of "Parents' Press", Berkeley, CA. His answer puts a basic tenet of Montessori philosophy into new words:

> *I think the most important value by far is to bring up children excited about helping other people, first in their family, and then other people outside. More than anything else, children want to help — it makes them feel grown up. That includes simple things like being able to set the table. Parents say, 'Oh, I can do it quicker myself,' but that misses the point. Children should be encouraged to help, to be kind and loving to other people. I think these are the spiritual values that are quite obvious, but we're not paying enough attention to them.*

*So many kids are brought up to think of themselves first. I've heard fathers say to their sons, 'You're in the world to get ahead, kid.' I want to demystify the idea of spirituality by showing that it comes down to specifics like helping your parents at home, or imagining how you can grow up to be a helpful person to the world, rather than focusing on making a big pile of dough, or achieving some position in a company.*

Anthropological studies from all over the world show that children can be taught any set of values that their parents and their group truly believe in. If children worship material success rather than truth or compassion, it is because they have absorbed those values from others. We should not let children grow up believing that they are in the world primarily to acquire possessions or to get ahead. If we give them no spiritual values to live by, they are wide open to the materialism pounded in by television programs, music videos and other commercial hucksterism.

In Montessori schools the ages in groups of children always span at least three years, age 1-3, 3-6, 6-12, 12-15, and so on. This is vital because in such natural, family-like groups children learn to help each other, teach each other, ask for help, observe to see if they are needed, to be responsible for others, and to feel good about themselves. Unlike the situation in a family, where one will always be "the first child" or the "middle child", this child gets to move from being the youngest to being the oldest.

The kindergarten year in a Montessori preschool, or the sixth grade of an elementary class is magical for a child. It is in these years, when being the oldest children, that the generosity and responsibility that Dr. Spock talks about above comes to fruition and these spiritual values become part of the child's being.

# THE LOVING ACT OF FATHERING

*Dear Susan,*

*I am married and have two children, 2 1/2 years old, and 4 months old. I work twenty hours a week outside the home. My husband, who is temporarily disabled, shows no interest or concern in helping with the childcare. When I go to work he drops the children off at his mother's. When I am home, he leaves all the caretaking to me. I have to attend to all of the chores as well as just caring for the children. How can I help my children grow up healthy even though their father seems so uninterested? How can I help my children to understand healthy male/female relationships, even though they obviously don't witness one?*

— Anonymous


Dear Anonymous,

I think you have asked one of the most important parenting questions there are: "How can I help my children to understand healthy male/female relationships?" It is in these first few years of life that children learn just what it means to be a human being, to be a friend or partner, to communicate with other human beings. They learn this first from the people in their home, not from what we say, but what we do. The fact that you are interested in providing a healthy model means that you already understand this.

The title uses the word "fathering" but families come in all kinds and the important point is that there should be a "second adult" in the child's life. This can be a mother, a partner, but not a nanny, because this second person should be someone who will be in the child's life forever.

Let me give you some suggestions based on Montessori experience. We know that children need and love challenges that they can work on diligently. It is the daily, selfless, giving, work, and concentration, in Montessori classes that produce the phenomenon of loving, happy, "normal" children, as opposed to those exhibiting various temporary deviations. It is the same with adults. When we give of ourselves, and work toward the good of something or someone else, we "love" the object of our effort—be it charity work, job, our children, or our spouses. Real love is not just a word, but an action; it is not to be confused with awakening hormonal adolescent emotions, or physical attraction.

When we first begin to live with a partner, before having children, we have a lot of time to think of this person's needs, to give to and so we "love" this person. With the coming of children we often expect this partner love to thrive without any time or effort spent, but our love is given to those new things, which require our time and effort. This always requires an adjustment.

You are fortunate to have a mother-in-law who is able and willing to care for the children. I imagine that she would be willing to do this on a weekly basis to help you and your husband have time to nurture your relationship—for the benefit of your children, and then their children, and their children—for you will be creating a family pattern of valuing human relationships which will be modeled through generations.

I have often pondered the fact that we spend many years being educated for a profession, but are expected to know how to be a good and happy parent, wife, or husband with no training at all. A good 10-session, do-it-yourself course, which gives direction to this valuable time and effort, and is fun and very rewarding, is presented in *Getting the Love You Want*, a book by Harville Hendrix. We have used it in our family, as a couple, and with our children.

A friend in Mongolia put it wisely:

*A wedding is just the beginning of the journey and all journeys take effort and time to be successful.*


My husband has a message for your husband:

*We men are often afraid to be with our children at first, afraid that we will not know what to DO. We do not have to 'do' anything in the beginning but to watch them, to be with them completely — without reading, watching TV, looking at our phone, or any other distraction — to focus on them and discover who they are. Even when we sit down to read a book with a child each time will be unique.*

# POWER AND OBEDIENCE

*Dear Susan,*

*My husband and I have a disagreement about obedience; he expects absolute compliance with commands, where I see that sometimes our children are deeply involved in an activity that makes them hesitate. Does obedience come only through fear of the power of the adult?*

— A Reader

Dear Reader,

First I would like to say that there are many different kinds of parenting and it is not helpful for one parent to tell the other that he or she is correct and the other is not. In some areas parents will agree, and in some there will be differences. The child will learn that there are many ways for his adults to love and guide him.

In this case I think your husband is correct in believing that children must learn to comply absolutely with commands. But one should not issue too many, or unnecessary, commands. Be sparse with them.

I would say rather that true obedience comes only through trust in the power of the adult, the power of the adult to protect the child. A child feels a great security and safety in knowing that his or her parent is in charge. If a child starts to touch a hot stove or run out into the street and the parent says "no", the child must know that "no" means "stop what you are doing." If "no" is used all day long for little things the child will stop paying attention.

There are some important things to keep in mind in teaching the child to obey. Among these are the age and developmental stage of the child, how this lesson is taught, how often a parent should command, and when he or she should command.

When a child is under the age of three there is a strong contact with inner drives to develop, mentally and physically. This child can only do what this inner guide dictates. To develop healthily a child needs to talk, move, climb, experiment, touch, and so on. Redirection is the key at this age. If the child is starting to climb on the dining room table, take the child to a place where climbing is okay. If the child is talking non-stop in church, or at a performance, take him out of the room to a place where he can keep talking.

The message must be clear to the child. When it becomes necessary to completely stop an action instead of redirecting it, make the message clear. If the child is reaching for an electric outlet, pick him up and gently remove him as you say the word "no." Don't shout "no" and then wait expectantly, as if daring him to reach again. In the first instance the lesson, or the message, is "stop the activity." In the second it is "I am expecting you to disobey me, and I am getting mad at you." In this second example the child becomes confused and fearful and might think, "Does he want me to stop reaching, or to reach again? Which thing will make my dad stop being mad at me?" Obedience that comes about only through fear is temporary, and is not a very good preparation for life.

Consider carefully the number and frequency of your orders or commands. It is always helpful to put ourselves in our child's place when we are trying to decide on a tactic of child rearing. If the parent only commands when necessary for example during a walk saying, "stay out of the street," a child will always pay attention. If orders are handed out all day long, how is the child to know when to take them seriously? Instead this child learns to ignore them all.

To begin to break this constant-command habit, it is helpful for parents to examine their daily language, to try to use non-directive statements like "dinner is ready" instead of "come and eat", or choices like "do you want your milk in a cup or a glass" instead of "drink your milk".

When should one command or order a child? You are absolutely right in your intuition to respect the deep involvement of your children in activities. When children are concentrating, focusing, deeply involved in work for a part of each day, they become calmer, friendlier, and much easier to live with. Watching to see what a child is doing before speaking is a way of showing the respect due to any person, young or old.

# STRESS AND CHILDREN

*Dear Susan,*

*We are at our wit's end. Our son, age seven, is in a new private school and having a terrible time. School parents are complaining that he is bothering the other children, criticizing and insulting them, lying, and using terrible language. He had the same problem at his last school. He watches television a lot and the teacher thinks this might be part of the problem, but we have a lot of stress in the family and we all find relief in television. Do you really think that watching television could make that much difference?*

— Ready to try anything

Dear Ready,

Yes, for some children television (and now computers and tablets) can indeed be the main culprit. A few years ago the son of some of our best friends was diagnosed as hyperactive. He was sleepwalking, unable to concentrate, even violent. The family only watched television a few hours a week but they decided to remove it completely from their lives to see what would happen. Within a couple of weeks all of their son's negative behavior disappeared. After a short while they brought the TV back into the house but allowed him to watch only "Mister Rogers' Neighborhood" for a half of an hour a day. Immediately all of the negative behavior returned.

I do not mean to say anything against Mr. Rogers. His was one of the best shows on television for young children. But it seems that some children are affected by television — psychologically and physically — more than we know. Until the final results are in it seems preferable to completely remove screens from the life of such a child and find out for ourselves what the sensitivity level is.

But screens probably cannot explain all of these problems. You mentioned that there is a lot of stress in the family at the moment. There is a saying "Heal the parents and the children will heal themselves." Children of this age are sponges, not only of the language and customs of their family and culture, but of the emotions. It does no good to pretend with children that everything is all right when it is not. They feel the underlying feelings even more strongly when we try to hide them.

New parents often try to improve their everyday language, or their way of speaking to each other, when their babies get old enough to imitate them but children are studying us from the first day of life.

When a child listens to a parent talking on the phone and hears the parent profess to be sick to get out of something, and the child knows the parent is not telling the truth, the child learns that lying is okay. If a child is ordered around and criticized continually, guess how the child will act with others?

In our own home, we once went through periods of frustration because our son was constantly interrupting us while we were speaking, reading, or working. Then we realized that we had gotten back into the habit of interrupting him in the same fashion; we had taught him, by example, that interrupting others is acceptable behavior. Children are definitely our teachers, and our mirrors. Your child may be teaching you that it is time to heal yourselves, for your child's sake.

It is quite true that children learn what they live, and they treat others the way they are being treated, but in times of stress, it is asking a lot of parents to provide the calm, loving and polite models that we all desire to be. Don't be too hard on yourself, but do have a look at the moment-by-moment life of the family to see where you can start to make little changes to improve the daily quality of your own lives. And your son will benefit.

# MONTESSORI PHILOSOPHY AND SHOPPING WITH CHILDREN

*Dear Susan, What can I do, if anything, when a parent is being abusive to a child in our store?* — A local retailer

Dear Local Retailer,

This is a frustrating situation for everyone. Keep in mind that if one verbally criticizes a parent for his/her actions this can result in frustration and guilt and anger and the child will suffer too. This is because the parent is already stressed out and taking it out on the child for some reason, and hearing criticism is only going to make the parent feel worse. A better approach might be to always keep in mind the old saying "We are all doing the best we can with the information we have at the moment" and to see if there is something you can do to reduce the parent's stress level. An offer to hold the baby or entertain the child can sometimes give the message that the stress of the parent is recognized and also that the result of this problem has been observed.

Here are some points to consider this situation from the parent's point of view.

The Montessori approach would be to figure out how to prevent such a scenario by checking the child's needs with the preparation of the environment. The following points might be helpful to parents and to retailers:

1- All children need to move, to touch, and to explore. They are not created to hold still and be quiet at this age. If they are in a situation where this is not allowed the parent could prepare by taking something along for them to work on—crayons, paper, a toy or puzzle, a small tape recorder. As a new mother I quickly learned that keys and other interesting objects carried in one's purse are a great help in just such emergencies. Depending on the size of my purse I sometimes carried a small artist sketchbook. We have several in our home, saved over the years that contain a delightful record of our children's drawings, tic-tac-toe games, etc.

The best way to take children into a place where it might be difficult for them to be "healthy and normal" is to go with one's partner or an adult friend. With this arrangement the adults can take turns, one doing the shopping or other errands, and one being completely available to the child or children.

2- Children quite naturally push parents to the limit. This is not being "bad"; it is merely research to find out exactly what the limits are. If parents are not careful they will teach their children that limits or rules of behavior are different at home than they are in public. This creates confusion for the child who then has to test and re-test the limits. For example, if a child starts to touch the stove at home, and the parent calmly says "no" and gently picks up the young child and moves him or her across the room, this gives a clear message that "no" means "move away from the object." In a store however the same parent is busy with other things and when the same child reaches for an item that he should not touch, and the distracted parents might say, "no" without having the time to remove the child. The child then gets the message that "no" in the store means "go on touching and the parent will say 'no' ten times and finally blow up." Or maybe it means, "go on touching and the parent will say 'no' five times and finally let you play with it." Researching and testing these changing rules is fascinating mental work for a child. The parent feels pushed to the limits, but the child just wants to know exactly what the rules ARE!

When one says that a parent should be consistent this is an example of what that means.

Okay, back to what the storeowner can do. This is based on experience in our own Michael Olaf Montessori store in the 1980's and 1990's in the San Francisco area:

When a child and parent or adults walked in the door, the first thing they saw was the play area, which was almost completely enclosed with a low wall made by low bookcases. There was a low adult chair, so an adult could sit and talk with the child, or where a mother could nurse a baby. There was a low table and chairs, a child-size carpet sweeper, and a full-length mirror. There was a book display containing books of interest to a wide age range of children, and several low wooden shelves, with paper and crayons and one or two puzzles and toys, neatly arranged with enough space to make them beautifully inviting.

The adults who work in the store checked the area throughout the day to be sure that the play area was straightened up, and they sometimes would invite a child to help them neaten it. The part of the store that was off limits to children was clearly marked, and parents who had missed seeing the play area as they entered the store were invited to make use of it, usually to their great relief. We were lucky to have the space to create this. Sometimes a mother would stop in just to nurse her baby and that was fine. We knew she would come back and shop as the child grew up.

A valuable investment is an available bathroom. This and a play area will give your store a reputation for being child-friendly, family-friendly. So first of all you must decide if you want that kind of reputation and patronage.

Even with the most carefully arranged environment and the best efforts of the parent, we have to consider just how much time a child can happily spend in a strange environment. In the past, and in some cultures today, children had time to think and to process sensorial input from such new experiences. They had more time to play in the sand or with blocks, do puzzles, take walks, to read, or to do other peaceful and real work around the house on which they could focus and concentrate.

During times like these a child can focus on processing information gained during new experiences, to figure things out and make sense of the world. Today children seem to have more rushed, intense lives, full of input that needs to be processed, classes, play-dates, television, computers, being driven from place to place, school, more driving, lessons, driving, shopping, iPad, radio, and more television.

What they desperately need is time to process all of this input. It is comforting for parents to realize that rushing from place to place every day is often a habit that can be changed when we examine our lives to discover what is essential and what is not. Parents can come to realize that they do not have to orchestrate every moment of their children's day. It is sometimes absolutely necessary to be in a child-unfriendly situation, but with practice we can all reduce stress in our lives by limiting these experiences, and learning to handle them with grace.

# HOW YOUR CHILD IS INTELLIGENT

Dear Susan,

*My seven-year-old cousin is having trouble with retention of math concepts. He is very strong in athletics and is very social. Could you suggest some help that I could give to his parents. Thank you.*

— Erin Anderson


Dear Erin,

Montessori practice is well known for meeting the needs of various learning styles or different kinds of "intelligences" and this applies to math.

Since the publication of Harvard psychologist Howard Gardner's book, *Frames of Mind: The Theory of Multiple Intelligences* in 1983, educators have begun to expand upon the traditional linguistic and logical-mathematical teaching methods (listen, speak, read, write, math), and to appreciate other kinds of intelligences. Thomas Armstrong has published, *In Their Own Way*, which translated the seven kinds of intelligence into seven "personal learning styles." Learning math is one of the examples he gives — learning math in seven different ways! You might want to share this book with the parents. I was very fortunate to take a class from Dr. Gardner at Harvard and to be interviewed by Thomas Armstrong as he prepared to write his book. But I keep learning about kinds of intelligence to this day.

From what you say about your cousin my first thought is that he may benefit from learning with large body movements — adding and subtracting basketballs on the lawn for example (bodily-kinesthetic intelligence), and then linking the math problem carried out with the basketballs to one on paper. And he might learn well with a small group of children — two or three doing the basketball math together (interpersonal intelligence).

When our son was younger he always walked in a circle if he was explaining something about which he was terribly excited. When he first began to read aloud he carried his book and walked this same circle. This is an example of bodily-kinesthetic intelligence. I sometimes wonder what would have happened to his excitement and enthusiasm if he had been made to sit still at these times.

Here is a brief description of each of the seven kinds of intelligence, and suggestions for ways of approaching math. Every person has a bit of each kind of intelligence, and more than one is used at a time. Strength in one kind of intelligence can be used to lead a child to develop strength in the others, if supportive materials and activities are available in the environment.

### *Logical-mathematical intelligence*

This person enjoys traditional ways of using the mathematical mind — discerning logical or numerical patterns, handling logical steps in reasoning. Materials and activities might include, strategy games (chess, checkers, Go), logic puzzles, science kits, computer programming software, nature equipment, brainteasers,

Cuisenaire rods and other concrete math materials, and detective games.

### Linguistic intelligence

This person learns through listening, reading, and speaking. Math materials and activities might include listening to multiplication tapes, then memorizing and repeating or chanting. Be sure and value the person's skill at imaginative storytelling, talking, books, writing materials, discussions, debates, and public speaking as well as math.

### Musical intelligence

Take advantage of the skill to produce and appreciate rhythm, by chanting multiplication tables for example, or chanting other math concepts. Memory games such as "Thirty days hast September . . . " There is a lot of math involved with developing musical skills with percussion instruments, metronomes, computerized sound systems, reading and writing music.

### Bodily-kinesthetic intelligence

This person has the ability to control one's body movements and to handle objects skillfully. He might be like our son, who learned academic subjects more easily when moving around the room rather than sitting still at a desk. Concrete math materials that are moved around are especially useful for this person. Be sure to validate the abilities of sports, and ways of learning any subjects through manipulating objects and moving.

### Spatial intelligence

This person learns math concepts, or anything else, by use of pictures. Both creating them and looking at them. In the world of math materials and activities can include films, slides, videos, diagrams, charts, maps, art supplies for creating beautiful images, graphic design software, three-dimensional building supplies (Legos), and drafting materials

### Interpersonal intelligence

These people are naturals at working well in groups, making up math challenges, story problems for their friends. Researching the history of these subjects in a group would help this person process and master math concepts, and maybe become interested in learning more. Materials and activities: cooperative learning, interactive software, group games, discussions, group projects, simulations, and peer teaching

### Intrapersonal intelligence

This person is a self-directed learner, skilled at setting and reaching goals. Materials and activities: self-paced instruction, individualized projects, places to retreat to and privacy to think—forts, tree houses—diaries and journals, even meditation.


The most important use of this information, in my opinion, is that it helps parents realize that every child is gifted in some way, and to appreciate the uniqueness of each child.

# TELEVISION!
# PASSIVE OBSERVATION OF LIFE

*Dear Susan, Our children seem to prefer watching television over anything else. I worry about their health and their eyes. What can we do?*

—Tired of TV

Dear Tired,

Your question addresses not only television but also computers, which are programmed to be addictive, for both children and adults. It is a very important question.

In the 1950s ours was the first family in our small town in Indiana to have a television and I have very fond memories of Howdy Doody and The Mickey Mouse Club, but there was nothing worth watching for more than two or three hours a week. We were lucky. Today the average child watches three or more hours a day of television, or spends this amount of time on a computer. This time is stolen from the highest quality of life's experiences—thinking, walking in nature, making music, talking and laughing together as a family, gardening, building, baking, visiting with and helping friends and neighbors, painting, enjoying leisurely family meals, and so on . . .

Here is a quote from Dr. Silvana Montanaro, MD, and a psychiatrist, Rome, Italy:

> *Television, contrary to what we are led to believe, is an anti-experience and an anti-knowledge machine because it separates individuals from themselves and from the environment and makes them believe they are living while they are only observing passively what other people decide to make them see.*
>
> *The negative effect of television on young children shows clearly at school time. Primary teachers report a significant decline in the manual abilities of five and six-year-olds. During the first years of life handwork is crucial for the development of the brain.*

And another from Urie Bronfenbrenner, Professor of Human Development, Cornell University

> *The primary danger of the television screen lies not so much in the behavior it produces as the behavior it prevents... Turning on the television set can turn off the process that transforms children into adults.*

We are learning more all the time about the negative effects of television — hyperactivity, aggressive behavior, desensitization, fear, obesity, ill health, violence, dishonesty, and immorality similar to that modeled on soap operas and talk shows. The thousands of commercials children are exposed to have had a terrible influence throughout the world. Like our family some have moved "to the country" to give our children a gentle childhood and more time in nature, but with television we may have brought the worst part of our culture to the country with us.

Those of us adults who are addicted to this passive activity find it very difficult to completely remove it from our homes. If you would really like to go "cold turkey" with TV I can recommend this book, written years ago but still valuable, *Four Arguments for the Elimination of Television*.

If this is too drastic a step for your family, let me quote Dr. Montanaro again:

> *Television should ideally be viewed with adults who can comment on it and guide children to a more conscious understanding of what they are seeing. We should make it possible for children to collaborate with us as soon as they can walk well so they are busy in real activities... read together, play cards or chess, paint, and ...talk! The family is the first place where children must live the values we say we believe in. In the family begins the transformation of society.*

# GOOD BOOKS FOR CHILDREN

*Dear Susan,*

*Our daughter is at the in-between age, thirteen, ready for more challenging reading. She enjoys history, biography, and nonfiction. Andrea loves to read. Do you have any suggestions?*

—Sheila Lovio, Humboldt State University

Dear Sheila,

If Andrea loves to read you have been successful in one of the most important parts of her education. Here are some ideas based on what Montessori schools suggest for a young person of this age, and some specific suggestions for books.

Following Interests: Montessori teachers try to keep a very small book collection of very beautiful and inspiring books at the school. They prefer to aid the child's exposure to the best library available. Watch to see what Andrea becomes interested in from day to day and help her learn to carry out research in the public library. If she reads a news article about an animal virus, for example, and has some questions, she may initially look up that particular virus in the library catalog, go to that shelf, and end up exploring many other areas, opening up new worlds of interest—the history of microscopes, the discovery of the yellow fever vaccine, the building of the Panama Canal, the anatomy of mosquitoes, the problem of babies with Zika . . . who knows what.

In our Northern California community, as I search for a particular book I cannot walk through the rows and rows of bookshelves without gathering books in my arms that I had never noticed before. This could be the same for your daughter. Whenever possible you might schedule more time than it takes to return a book and look for a particular title, for such exploration.

It is good to create a basic home library. When families first begin to take young children to a library, or to buy books, they usually tend to focus on fiction. Fiction versus non-fiction is a major topic in Montessori philosophy. Children under the age of six are intent on figuring out how the real world works. They want the truth, stories about how we parents and grandparents lived as children, facts about which birds eat which food, the names of fruits and vegetables, how a house is built, or how cotton grows and is turned into clothing. They will listen to anything a parent will read to them but we do them a disservice if we do not feed this interest in the real world at this age.

At library visits and home collections we can find interesting books about countries, famous people, plants, animals, music, art, sports, crafts, astronomy, and all of the other nonfiction areas, for children from a very young age. It is a good idea to have one or two from several areas of knowledge in the home. I would stay away from textbooks because they are usually written at the lowest level of comprehension, and in a pretty boring style- certainly with no sense of humor! A good one-volume, colorful science of biology encyclopedia (and there are many available today) will raise a lot of questions and send a child off to the library for answers.

Book Reports and Discussions: Many Montessori schools use the Great Books program to introduce the great classics of literature. But I have heard teachers say that if a book report or a discussion is required children soon lose their natural love of reading and tend to go through books in an analyzing and critical way — the opposite of curling up in front of the fire for a good read.

My Montessori elementary, age 6-12, teacher trainer recommended, and then I used to recommend, giving a book a 50-page trial. Then, if the child doesn't like it, try another. Literary discussions, analysis, and original writing will arise spontaneously from the children, but they shouldn't be imposed.

In our home we have had several collections of abridged classics with a lot of pictures and a short brief version of the story that have inspired our children to later read the originals. There are two recent books full of suggestions of books to introduce to children and to young adults. These are *Books That Build Character*, by Kilpatrick and Wolfe, and *The Book of Virtues* by Bennett.

Some personal suggestions of fiction books from our family library are *Jane Eyre* (Charlotte Bronte), *My Antonia* (Willa Cather), *The Chosen* (Chaim Potok), *The Chronicles of Narnia* (C.S. Lewis), *Jonathon Livingston Seagull* (Richard Bach), *The Lord of the Rings Trilogy* (J.R.R. Tolkein), *A Story Like the Wind* and *A Far-off Place* (Laurens van der Post) and books by George

MacDonald, Francis Hodgson Burnett, Sigrid Undset, and too many biographies and nonfiction books to mention. Enjoy!

(NOTE: A good quality set of encyclopedias will remain valuable for the home and classroom. Research shows that getting a quick answer to a question by Googling it is very different than picking up a book, leafing through the pages or looking through the index, finding the page, and sorting through the words to construct your own answer. In the second instance, holding a book in one's hands, the information is retained far longer. Perusing the pages of an encyclopedia can be just like looking through the shelves in a library.)

## TEENAGE TROUBLE

*Dear Susan,*

*My teenage daughter has been acting like a two-year-old. What's going on?*

—Name withheld for obvious reasons

Dear Name Withheld,

You have no idea how common this question is. Adults who are interested in teaching Montessori at the middle and high school level find that the birth-to-age-three, or Assistants to Infancy Montessori training is the one that helps them the most because it covers the formation of the personality. Age 0-3 is the foundation of childhood. And age 12-15 is the foundation of adulthood. Age 0-3 and 12-15 have a lot in common. They are both periods of extremely rapid growth and development, physically and in other ways, and there is a definite push-pull relationship with parents and other adults. At times the child or young person wants to be hugged and babied and a moment later wants to be completely independent and respected as an equal.

Do you remember the "terrible twos"? If we as adults understand the need for expressing oneself, making decisions, making mistakes, and growth, this period can actually be the "wonderful twos". There is a parallel in the teenage years.

Joseph Chilton Pearce offers us help in understanding the needs of the adolescent in his book *Evolution's End*:

> *Adolescence is an arbitrary, contrived category. In past eras children were children until the early teens wherein, through some rite of passage, they were ushered into and took their place in adult society. Today there is no economic place for young adults and no rites of passage. We have, instead, created a holding stage that keeps young people in a limbo, into which children enter earlier and adults stay longer year-by-year.*
>
> *Social needs are intense during this period, so this excluded group forms its own subculture based on models that ostensibly stand against the main culture and 'for' the alienated young. These models are carefully engineered for commercial exploitation of this age group (beauty, clothing, music, cars, etc.).*

*Like the underground in the novel 1984, this counter culture is produced by the culture.*

*The resulting generation gap is equally a new phenomenon in history. In previous times young people wanted to take part in adult life and looked forward to plunging in to 'prove themselves'. Throughout history the young have followed the footsteps of their elders, and created history. The word 'discipline', from the word 'disciple', a follower, meant 'to follow the exemplar'. A break down in discipline in young people is a break down in our genetically encoded agenda for following the model. A rebellious adolescent refusing or reluctant to take his or her part in society is a biological anomaly.*

Does this help? As Montessori children around the world reach this age and stage of development there is a lot of research being shared. The program *The Adolescent Orientation* program has even become an official AMI Montessori teacher-training program. In the meantime perhaps the best thing we can do, is to look at our children in this new light and to try to help them find ways to contribute to society, to do real work. We can talk to them about the gap between society's expectations of adolescence in the past and in the present. And above all we can try our best to give them unconditional love—loving them exactly the way they are—as they go through this tumultuous time of life.

# TEACHING CHILDREN
# TO MANAGE THEIR TIME

*Dear Susan,*

*Thank you for the opportunity to ask questions in your column. The most valuable advice you gave to me last year was to speak to the children as I would to an adult. I began noticing when I was being disrespectful to them and it completely changed my attitude. The respect given over the year changed them. They were respectful of me and I felt free to be myself rather than some "lord of the room."*

*Your other point that helped the most was the idea of not doing for them anything they can do for themselves. I began thinking about our day and what was being done for them.*

*Here is a list of some of the things that they took over: taking attendance, choosing weekly jobs, checking them, posting the schedule, making certain materials, distributing papers to parent folders, helping with tasks in the school office, going to the store (with an adult) to buy classroom supplies, handling the "book orders", letting them choose when to have recess, then going out when they were ready, not having to wait for the whole class.*

*Susan, now I have another question. I see myself lately as an instructor in "time management". Do you have suggestions for helping children plan and execute their own work? Thank you.*

—Katherine O'Brien, Elementary Montessori teacher, Rochester, Minnesota

Dear Katherine,

Thank you for your question. I think it is of interest, not only to schools, but also to parents and children at home. Teaching your students time management and responsibility for their own work is vital preparation for life. It used to be very clear what a child or young person had to learn in order to succeed in life, thus the standard academic curriculum was universal. But because of the speed at which the world is changing, that is no longer the case.

It is impossible for a teacher or administrator today to design a subject-matter-based curriculum for an elementary student with the assurance that it will be useful when that student graduates from high school. It is much better for parents, teachers, and administrators to help a child learn to discover and solve problems, to learn how to plan and execute work projects, set and meet goals, learn how to work with others, to help and teach others, to discover their unique talents and abilities, and to do research.

The following steps should help with your time Management goals.

1- Make a list, having the children help with this if possible, of the basic requirements for each grade year — no more than one page for each year. By requirements I mean bare bones, such as "long division" or "capitalization rules", whatever is required in your state. The idea is to help them cover the basics and to free them for individually chosen work. If you do not have access to a public school list go to the best school, private or public, you can find, and ask for their suggestions as to what should be completed by the end of each grade year. Hang these in the classroom for all to see throughout the year. This should be a simple, manageable list, no more than one page per grade level.

2- Discuss with the children, in small groups, or individually, the fact that you want to help them accomplish as much as they can, to enjoy it, and to learn to plan and complete their own assignments and projects.

3- With the children or one child at a time, come up with schedule examples, and list them. These can be anything from "math first thing every morning" to "finish all requirements in the first month of school." Help each child make a plan—at first for a week, then maybe two weeks, even a month at a time, on which the student records the required work, and then the other areas the student wants to explore.

There is no right way to plan and execute work, but your constant help will be needed for some children so that they can develop good work habits. Anything not accomplished in the given period of time can be carried over to the next list in the beginning but there is great satisfaction in learning to complete everything planned!

4- Help the children complete goals that can be accomplished. It is this successful completion that inspires further effort and success. If the plan was too grand, for example "learn all the multiplication tables by Friday," help the child modify to "be able to write out all of the multiplication tables by Friday," which can be done in order and is much easier.

5- Remember the Montessori maxim, "The adult is in charge of the minimum, the child the maximum." It has been shown over and over that when children are inspired and choose their own work, they will set a much greater task than an adult would ever require. But if children are overwhelmed by requirements and assignments, everything will lose its flavor, and inspiration for maximum effort will be lost.

6- Prepare the environment so that the students are spending their school days in an intellectual "health food store", not a "junk food store." Over the years I have found that the state-required work took no more than 2-3 hours a week, and I never required scheduled, specific work of the children other than this. Most of the time in class is then spent exploring, planning projects, reading, exploring what has been provided, and every activity, all work, will be valuable.

7- Be careful not to make a schedule or to impose requirements (other than those required by the state) such as one hour of math each day or one hour of silent reading. This makes learning tedious. At the 3-6 level each morning there is an uninterrupted 3-hour work period with no scheduled lessons or required group activities. This work period expands, from three hours a day, to days and weeks at the elementary, age 6-12, level.

8- Help the children learn to teach each other and to design group projects and presentations. Discuss the problems and goals with the children and they will come up with surprising solutions. Teach them to practice the delivery of information when making a presentation, not just reading a written paper. Children love to learn these skills.

9- Try not to impose rules that you wouldn't impose on your contemporary — regulations about when to eat, where to sit, what to read, and so forth. The children may themselves see a need for such rules and may, with your help, decide how and when to impose them on their group. This is valuable socialization. The only adult-made rule necessary when all of the activities in the environment are valuable is "you must not disturb another person who is working" so the concentration of the already working children is not interrupted.

During my first year of teaching in a Montessori elementary class in the Virgin Islands, I had handpicked a library of fiction and nonfiction books. When the children found out that as long as they fulfilled their minimum state-required requirements (for the day or week, depending on their own time-management plan) they could read for as long as they wanted to. They were thrilled.

For three days they all read for about five hours a day. I worked on making language materials in order to stay our of their way, but gradually I began to doubt the philosophy of "trusting the intuition of the children."

On the fourth day, just as I was beginning to weaken in my resolve and think about gathering them for a lesson, half of the children went back to work, on maps, math problems, piano, all of the other work in the class.

The next day the rest joined them in non-reading activities. I was so glad that I hadn't stepped in and made a rule about "reading only for one hour after lunch" or something equally as boring and controlling! Shortly after this I shared my anxiety and my relief with them, and we had a great discussion, and a great laugh!

## HOLIDAY MEMORY MAKING

*Dear Susan,*

*Do you have any suggestions for gifts, holiday memory making, etc. for our four year-old? He doesn't seem to play much with the toys in his toy box and we are at a loss for new ideas. Thank you.*

— A Father, Petoskey, Michigan

Dear Michigan father,

Let me tell you about the fourth birthday of the son of good friends in Oakland a few years ago. He had a party together with several families and received some beautiful presents. Among them were blocks, action figures, books, and I don't remember what else.

But what I DO remember is the look on his face when he opened the carpet sweeper we had given him! He was thrilled. It was a real adult carpet sweeper, in the smallest size, with a four-section handle, which could be made the correct height for a 4-year-old. The parents had to take it out of the packaging, assemble the handle immediately and he was using it on the carpet and the wood floor within minutes. A few days later the mother began scattering the wood shavings from the pencil sharpener on the carpet so he could find something to sweep up—because he had cleaned every inch of the floor.

You might want to examine the life of your family and come up with some real "tools" like this carpet sweeper, which would involve your son in the work of the family.

Containers as gifts have always been a hit with our family. This includes wooden shelves, baskets, trays, boxes, and anything else that helps to organize the home environment—bedroom, kitchen, living room, front hall, garage, and so forth. We don't usually think of such things as gifts, but some children (not all) consider organizing and sorting their toys and belongings as much fun as playing.

Low hooks to put next to the front door for children's jackets, stools to sit on while tying shoes, shelves in the living room or bedroom to help organize books and toys, baskets for sorting Legos, blocks, beads, doll clothes, whatever toys the child already has, these all make excellent holiday gifts. Think of what a treat it is for an adult, after the holidays, to sit down and organize a postcard collection or an assortment of photos into a new photograph file box, or a picture album. Children sometimes feel the same way about getting their things organized.

Another holiday suggestion is to take the emphasis off of receiving and to concentrate on giving. At this age your son can certainly participate in the wrapping and card making, even if he hasn't been directly involved in making the gifts. We work on our own family "Christmas list" for months ahead of the season. This is the list of things to give to or do for other people. You could include him in the creation of a list of this kind. This can give rise to all kinds of unique ideas of goods and services that can be given. Some years we have made little puppets, candles, or tea mixes and spiced honey with pretty labels. These were very fulfilling because the children could participate equally with the adult in the creation of the gift.

Our second daughter was the world-class coupon artist. She spent days cutting out colored paper, writing, decorating and wrapping gift certificates and coupons for a variety of services such as foot rubs, dish washing, poetry readings, and later baby-sitting. Our son has given the gift of music in several ways, a good-bye concert for a young boy who was moving away from California, a piano concert, complete with program, for his grandparents and their friends while visiting them in Florida, and an annual 30-minute tape of talking and playing music, which he has been sending to friends and relatives since he was six.

One of the main functions of all human celebrations, baptisms, marriages, funerals, Christmas, and so forth, is to pass on the spiritual beliefs and wisdom of the community. Whatever your religion is, the belief in being good, celebrating the family, caring for others, and so forth will be passed on to a four-year-old, not by words, but by actions. He will remember the spirit of holiday celebrations with memories of creating, singing, making the home beautiful with decorations, lighting candles, praying, and working to make others happy.

Some other ideas are: stringing popcorn, cutting out paper snowflakes for the window, singing, reading children's stories of your religious tradition, doing nice things for friends and relatives, making and/or wrapping gifts together, making ornaments and paper chains, baking, lighting candles. These activities can take as few as five minutes, and as long as a weekend. The practice of writing "Thank-you" notes, drawings at this age, and later detailed and personal letters, is very important for children. This is a way to give back, to grandparents and friends who have given gifts to children, and children need our help to create opportunities to give to others. I am sure you will come up with your own ideas and I wish you the best of luck in your memory creations this year.

In our fast-paced lives it is important to keep in mind that our children need our time and attention more than bought presents. You might want to make a "holiday list" of things you would like to do with your son, and try to fit one of them into your holiday schedule every day or so. I'm sure he will remember these gifts more than any which he might receive under the tree.

# HOMESCHOOLING A LA MONTESSORI

*Dear Susan,*

*I plan on homeschooling my children. I would like to provide them with the proper materials, but would never be able to spend as much money for all the materials they would encounter in a Montessori school. I would like to know which materials would be considered most essential.*

— Ellen Tsadanidas, Princeton, NJ

Dear Ellen,

Montessori materials, made from polished wood, metal, and cloth, are extremely attractive and inviting to children. Because of the strong impression they make on parents visiting a Montessori school, they are often thought to be essential, but they are not! It is the training and ability of the adult that makes a good Montessori class.

A friend with whom I studied in London years ago spent her first year teaching in a small country school in Nova Scotia. She had no materials except "practical life" (cooking, building, sewing, cleaning, etc.) and language (books, homemade sandpaper letters and movable alphabet, picture cards). She later told me that this was her best teaching year.

Several years ago I taught at a private school in Lima, Peru and had a similar experience. With books, cleaning and art supplies, a guitar, and materials gathered from homes to do physics and botany experiments, we had such a wonderful Montessori class that I ended up providing teacher education to help the other teachers understand the basic principles of Montessori.

Many people have taken Montessori teacher training for the main purpose of being better parents. And of these many went on to become teachers of other children because they loved the work (and because there are many job openings for well-trained Montessori teachers today!). If you want to use Montessori principles for homeschooling I suggest that you focus more on the theory and practical suggestions. These ideas are based on common sense parenting and teaching.

### Montessori Teaching Principles for the Home:

1- Prepare the environment to help children to act, and think independently, and make intelligent decisions, for example a mattress on the floor for a baby to get in and out of bed independently, low hooks for hanging up towels, pajamas, coats, etc., materials and books always ready for the child to choose.

2- Analyze in detail the steps in an activity or task that you want to help your child to master into manageable sections. Each mastered step provides a sense of accomplishment and prepares for the next stage. For example show a young child how to place only the napkins on the table when first learning to set the table for a meal, then the silverware, maybe vases of cut flowers, until over several weeks the child can learn to set the whole table. In another example learning to assemble knobbed puzzles prepares a hand for learning to hold a pencil properly, because the knobs prepare the hand to correctly hold a pencil. Create a game of "putting things away" and "cleaning up after a project," separate from the rest of the work.

3- Have patience, take time, try to respect concentration - even if it is only that of a child trying to put on a sweater, or building with blocks. It is the choosing and enjoying the task, and the focus and concentration that are important, not the perfection of the activity.

4- Guidelines for Materials: I do not know the ages of your children, but at all ages I would say that essential materials are those which have a real practical purpose, allow the child to move, and have exact techniques which the child can master - cooking, sewing, gardening, playing a musical instrument, science experiments, for example - math and language will be more successful, no matter what materials are used, if the child has developed concentration, careful work habits, completion of cycles of work, cleaning up after himself, responsibility, solving problems, and making decisions. Materials should be as beautiful and inviting as you can afford, made of natural materials instead of plastic.

Think about all of the areas of learning - botany, zoology, art, music, physics, geology, literature, math, etc. Find a few inspiring books or activities to introduce the child to each area. Then help facilitate further research in the interest of the moment. Try to have a special place for each book and piece of material so that it can always be found when the child is inspired to work, even labeling the shelves if this helps your family — it helps ours, especially in our library.

To reemphasis the point that the environment, the adult, the work of the child are all more important than the materials, let me share with you a favorite quote:

> . . but I know happiness does not come with things. It can come from work and pride in what you do.
>
> — M. Gandhi

I have published two books that would be helpful to anyone asking for this help today. They are *The Red Corolla, Montessori Cosmic Education* (for 3-6) and *Montessori Homeschooling* (for kindergarten through high school).

## LEARNING TO LOVE HISTORY

*Dear Susan,*

*Can you tell me how history is taught in the Montessori system? All I remember of my school experience is hating to memorize dates. Later my husband and I traveled a bit and became enthralled with the history of countries we visited, but that method is impractical as far as sharing history with our children. They are 4 and 8. How can I help them learn to love history the way we do? Thank you.*

*— Reader*

Dear Reader,

Before the age of six children are in the "motor-sensorial" period of life. That means that they do not learn well while sitting still, but need to move around and to use all of their senses. Throughout the Montessori years, primary and elementary, geography and history are interrelated. You have found this to be true in your travels and I have also had this experience.

For both children you could play music from many different cultures, show pictures and provide objects to handle from different cultures. Cook simple ethnic foods with the children and sing songs, or at least listen to recordings of them, in the different languages. Creating and dressing up in ethnic costumes and eating ethnic foods is a wonderful preparation for history. This can be as simple as a sheet tied over the head and a lunch of dates for an Arabic experience, maybe inspired by a local belly-dancing performance.

At this age we focus on areas of human life children see every day and can relate to, such as food, shelter, clothing, and transportation. For the older child there will be an interest beyond these physical needs and an interest in the mental and spiritual needs, marriages, and how other celebrations have become part of a culture. The older child will begin to understand that we are all brothers and sisters and the differences in cultures (and thus history) arise first of all because the places and climates where humans live—deserts, jungles, mountains, coasts, etc.—are different. Constant reference to a globe reinforces all of these elementary of geography, and this becomes history.

A key principle in Montessori is to "follow the child." These "history" lessons are much more successful if they are offered in response to a question, an experience, or an interest of the child, rather than a timetable or lesson plan of the adult. If your child sees someone playing African drums, for example, and wants to know more about this culture, this is the time to dance to African music, cook couscous and look in the library for picture books of Africa. In this way you and your child will be searching together for something you both are already interested in. There is a saying "Neurons that fire together wire together." This explains the Montessori emphasis on learning by combining impressions and senses and relating subjects to each other.

If a parent or teacher decides, unrelated to an interest of a child, to give an "Eskimo lesson" you may have to spend most of the time entertaining or trying to interest the child and much of the experience can be lost. Very little is usually learned when the lesson begins with an interest of the adult rather than the child.

Do you have a regular time during which you read to your children? You might check out the nonfiction children's section of the library. There are some really well illustrated children's versions of historic novels and biographies. Any book that is interesting to the parent will be interesting to the child. There are some really well done picture biographies of famous artists, scientists, and so forth. If your child is especially taken with one, point out that country on the globe.

For the child from six to twelve years of age, Montessori schools have discovered that children need an overall picture first, and then the details, which they can fit into this broad overview.

From age 6-8 in Montessori schools the focus is on the creation of Earth and prehistoric life.

From age 8-10 it is on early humans and early civilizations, from tribal cultures to the development of cities. From age 10-12 the child's own national and state history is emphasized.

Can you see how being presented with the overall or broad picture first can help the following studies make sense and have a place to put the details? Because children in a Montessori class are mixed in ages from 6 - 12 and all of these experiences are going on all the time, the child can delve into any aspect of history at any time. An interest quite naturally flows into the other areas of study, such as math, language, and art.

For the older child, in a Montessori class the exposure to the study of history is as varied and interesting as for the younger. Children still study the physical needs of humans — food, transportation, shelter, and clothing, defense, religion, education, language and so on — but now they also study the mental and spiritual needs of humans. It is very interesting to discover how cultures have met these needs in different ways. Children see that cultures changed and evolved over the years and this naturally awakens an interest in historical timelines, looking for them in books, and sometimes making them. I saw an interesting timeline in a Montessori school in Rome, Italy on the process of making wine, from the planting of the vines to the pouring of wine into a glass. This definitely was inspired by an interest in one of the students, and reflects the culture of the moment.

You may find that your children want to express this new information by cooking, making up stories, working on ethnic arts and crafts, singing and dancing, even making timelines, maps, and charts. A child easily remembers the dates of an historical period when she has chosen to study it and has created something of her own.

In my opinion it is the quality of the experiences rather than quantity that is important. If you think back on what you remember about history in your life it was probably not a neatly laid out and planned curriculum of history lessons, and certainly not dates! It was people, experiences, interesting historical novels, the answers to your pressing questions, or a friend or teacher with a passion to share — and it sounds like you have the passion to share with your children.

# FUN WITH GREAT AUNT AND UNCLE

*Dear Susan,*

*My husband and I have no children but we have several nieces and nephews. One in particular, has a 2 1/2 year girl and a 6-month-old girl. What activities can we, as Great Aunt and Uncle, do with these young girls to enrich and enhance their development? The baby, obviously, isn't as interesting to us as the 2 1/2 year old who is potty trained and speaks.*

*— Reader*

Dear Reader,

For general information about children at this age, and to prepare for their next visit, I refer you to my book *The Joyful Child: Montessori, Global Wisdom for Birth to Three*. In order to answer your question I am thinking back to what I remember of visits to aunts and uncles, and grandparents in my own life. One of the things I remember with pleasure is having familiar places to which we returned each time. The tall climbing gym at a nearby schoolyard in Ft. Dodge, Iowa comes to mind. Familiar reference points to which one returns regularly help a child feel secure away from home. Climbing and playing on playground structures is very valuable for the development of young children.

Taking a walk at each visit, but always to the same place, will tune the child in to the changes in nature and the skill in observing nature will become more and more refined over the years. I remember a black walnut tree on my grandparents' farm in Indiana. The first time we went to this tree my grandmother and we children spread blankets underneath and our grandfather climbed up into the tree to shake out the walnuts. From then on visiting this tree was often included in our visits — to examine the buds, leaves, and flowers, as we witnessed the end of the yearlong production of nuts.

Looking forward to familiar foods is a fun part of visiting relatives. We always visited the Iowa family at peach season and there was never a time when we were not welcomed with the smell of fresh baked angel food cake, served with fresh peaches and whipped cream. The other grandmother always made noodles for us. A large "noodle" (about 15 inches in diameter) would be hanging over the backs of each chair in the kitchen, drying. Within a few hours we would wash our hands, put on aprons, roll up the large noodles, cut them into strips, and lay them out on the kitchen table for further drying — looking forward to setting the table for chicken noodle soup for dinner.

The grandparents we visited most often had only a few children's books and toys but they were very special. There was a six-volume set of books called *My Bookhouse* by Olive Beaupré Miller, published in 1920. These books contained nursery rhymes, fantasy stories, myths, and historical and biographical tales, opera, and poetry, adventure — for children from birth through high school. Today even the sight of one of the illustrations from these books brings back wonderful memories, and I have collected complete sets over the years, one for each of our children. There are many variations of these books available today and you could easily start a carefully selected library of your own.

These grandparents also had a very few toys, but they were made of wood, and each had a special place on a shelf in the closet under the stairs. There were dominos, Chinese checkers, and blocks. But mostly I remember the joy of having the undivided attention of these dear people as we played these games in the evenings and carefully put the toys back on the shelf, knowing that they would be there whenever I wanted to play with them. Today in our home we have a similar under-stairs closet with these things for our visiting grandchildren

When we went to bed at night our grandmother played music, on the harp or on the piano downstairs, while we went to sleep. Reading or singing or just putting soft music on the tape player would be a great way to enhance and enrich the development of your great nieces.

The relatives we visited always planned to devote time to us and they included us in their regular activities. My fondest memories of gardening, pulling weeds and picking peas were from these visits. Together we planted trees, did the laundry, made the beds, and took baskets of food to invalids. I think these are the best memories, the time taken to be with us and to share their lives. The best advice I can offer is for you and your husband to draw from your own happy memories and enjoy creating new ones with your nieces.

# NEPAL, Montessori for the Forgotten Himalayan Children

The Boudhanath area on the outskirts of Kathmandu, Nepal is on the ancient trade route from Tibet. Tibetan merchants have rested and offered prayers there for many centuries, and when refugees entered Nepal from Tibet in the 1950s, many decided to live around the Boudhanath stupa, one of the largest in in the world.

This was 2006. I was a guest of the Shree Mangal Dvip (SMD) Boarding School for poor village children throughout the country. A Tibetan Buddhist teacher had founded the School in 1987 and today it is completely funded by overseas sponsors in twenty-six countries. I was here to learn and to share.

Most evenings I would join a few of the high school students to walk the *kora*, a ritual of circumambulating the stupa three times while praying for peace and happiness for all. We joined pilgrims from around the world on this path. I can still hear the melody in my head of "Om Mani Padme", an ancient mantra related to the bodhisattva of compassion, the sounds of recordings being played in the shops.

On the way to and from the stupa the students and I discussed their life back in the villages, their school days, life and goals, and what I was learning from them and the others at the school. They had a lot to teach me. Without exception they wanted to learn all they could to return to help their communities.

Shirley Blair, a Canadian, and one of three heads of this school, had been introduced to Montessori through friends in Vancouver who recommended me as a consultant. She wanted to create a system of education that was modern, but still in line with the principles of the ancient cultures, creating balanced lives for the students. In learning about Montessori she realized that she also wanted the students to learn in a Montessori way, which she described accurately as, *cooperation over competition, compassion, peer teaching, enjoying learning, and caring for the environment.*

### Learning from the Students

I spent a week at the school, sleeping in one of the rooms in the teachers' quarters, eating with the children in the dining room, observing classes at all levels from preschool through high school, and, when the school day was over, spending time with the children, learning about their lives and hopes.

The sleeping quarters were very crowded with 3-tier bunk beds. Laundry was done by hand (sometimes by students, the older helping the younger, sometimes by *Amalas* or mothers working as support staff) and hung on the bunk beds or the railings outside the dorm rooms to dry.

The meals were very simple, *dal baht*, which means rice and lentils, at every meal, accompanied by Tibetan bread, greens, and often a piece of fruit. At the beginning of each meal a child, from the very youngest to the eldest, was selected (perhaps as a reward for being quiet) to stand on a bench and lead the group in a prayer of thankfulness.

Most of the students have come from the far-off villages of the Himalayas. When I asked how far from Kathmandu is their home, a typical answer was, "one day by bus and five days walking" or "one day by bus and eight days walking."

The villages are situated in geographically challenging and isolated areas at high altitude (as high as 14,000 feet). They are subject to climate extremes, and have no roads, electricity, running water, modern sanitation, phones or Internet, health care or schools.

There are many things the students loved and missed in leaving their villages, their families, but it was a previously unheard of opportunity for the children to come here and receive a modern education, while still practicing their traditional religion and values.

### Meeting with the Teachers to Make a Plan

At the end of the week I had pulled together an outline for a weekend workshop with all of the teachers.

As a consultant it is not helpful to just provide a list of things that are wrong. Just as in the Montessori classroom the best procedure is first to observe and to learn; I have never explored a culture that didn't have strengths and elements that are a potential gift to the rest of the world.

The workshop began with a brief introduction to Montessori, then I shared the best of what I had observed, and then together we discussed how some things could be more in line with Montessori principles.

In discussing Montessori education I presented the characteristics that are inborn — a natural love of learning and work, the need to move around and not sit still all day, the need to explore physically and mentally, a love of silence, and the healing results of deep concentration. I gave a brief overview of how Montessori education is carried out differently at different ages, before age six, between ages six and twelve, and beyond.

Then I shared some of the observations I had made during the week living at the school. There were many elements of daily life already in line with Montessori.

### Independence and Practical Life

Here is an example. This school has the very minimum of funds so the students themselves are in charge of a lot of the daily work, called *practical life* work in Montessori. Everyone helps with the cooking, setting table, cleaning up. The students were already very responsible and independent outside of class, much more so than children in Western cultures. Older students do their own laundry and help the younger children with their homework. The older students make sure that their own, and the clothing of others, are kept clean. Everyone is kept clean and healthy even though there is only one shower for 250 children!

I watched an older student stand at the door before a meal and quite seriously check the cleanliness of the hands of the younger students before they could enter to eat.

Some days it seems that I was visiting a well-organized planet completely populated with children, with very few adults in sight.

While I was there children from ten to fifteen years of age were in charge of many aspects of a dental clinic held by volunteer dentists from the United States each year. The dental volunteers use the school as home base to provide dental care for poor children in Kathmandu. These SMD students had proven themselves as capable for this by working in the school clinic for three years before being able to assist in the dental clinic.

So part of my workshop was to explain that when children take care of each other, were valuable in the daily life of the school, and involved with such important work — rather than focusing only on academics — they were more aligned with Montessori and preparing to be more fulfilled adults.

### Keeping the Traditions

Here is the goal of the school:

*To preserve the culture, language and Buddhist way of life of the Himalayas, and to give Himalayan children the tools to build a better future, so they can help their own people when they grow up.*

What exists in this school is one of the best examples of how to navigate people from an ancient culture meeting, and being educated, in the modern world.

In the homes of these children there was a solid Tibetan Buddhist tradition of taking care of each other and the environment. Even though the modern amenities were not to be found in the mountain villages where these children came from, for the most part there had existed sustainable communities for hundreds of years. In such communities everyone helps each other to build homes, plant and harvest crops, solve problems, give birth and grieve, celebrate the landmark events of life, and there is often a lot of time between the hard work for music and dance and celebration.

When young and old people come from such communities to places where they will be faced with television and runaway consumerism, money exchange replacing barter, and competition for work and for goods, the result can be very destructive, and sometimes even the school books do not reflect the culture. For example these children learn their subjects in three languages at one time — English, Tibetan, and Nepali.

The staff at SMD is well aware of this situation, and the focus is to help the children master a modern curriculum while at the same time keeping in touch with the all important traditions of the culture.

However the academic model for learning in the classrooms was very traditional, the students reading from assigned textbooks, teacher lecturing (often right from the books) or writing on the blackboard. Students repeated the teacher's words or copied them from the blackboard, all as a group. The curriculum and textbooks are prescribed by the national government of Nepal and the national exams are based on these studies.

### Our Workshop Topics

Together the teachers and I discussed the following elements of Montessori: cooperation rather than competition in learning, the importance of adults modeling behavior expected of the students, respecting concentration, and ways that students could gradually move toward independent work and research, following interests, and learning to teach each other.

I showed a Birth to Three video of children in Montessori Infant Communities in Japan and the USA. It made the potential for concentration and the resulting compassion toward others, even in the tiniest children, very clear. It was helpful because the materials for age 0-3 are simple so the staff could focus on the children's behavior. Everyone was surprised at the abilities of children so young to be able to carry out long and involved activities such as washing dishes, and to see how they cared for the environment, and the kind way they treat each other.

The Vice Principal, a professional educator from India, was so inspired by the DVD that he told his son what these children could do and invited me to lunch with the family. Then the son immediately looked for ways to improve his own independence at home.

Then I shared the article I had written after teaching in a private girls' school in Lima, Peru. Together we discussed what could be changed immediately and what could be thought about for the future.

One day I took two high school girls with me to the Tibetan Refugee Center, which I had visited in 2003, the year I was helping Diptee Acharya plan the first Montessori school in the area. I encouraged the girls to interview the doctor who cares for the arriving Tibetans who are often suffering from severe frostbite and other injuries. They talked to the children who had arrived in the recent weeks. They also sat in on a discussion among four of the international media reporters who regularly come to the reception center to interview arriving refugees, because this is the only source of true and up-to-date information about what is going on in the Tibetan area of China.

On the way home the two SMD students begged me to stop at an Internet cafe so they could research this situation. I was more than happy to support this interest and pay for the Internet time. They were so excited to be encouraged to follow their curiosity that they asked the head of the school the next day if they could give a presentation to the whole school about their "Montessori Day."

This was a first for the school and the principal was pleased. He turned to me and said, "Is this Montessori education?" He called a meeting of the girls and their teachers, Shirley and I were invited, and they all discussed the possibility of giving permission for the girls to do research and make a presentation, at length.

As a result of the discussions along the lines of, "If we let the girls decide what they are going to study, what will happen with the rest of the students!" their request was denied. But the fire had been lit. The girls would continue their interest. And the teachers would think of student-centered possibilities.

I spoke at length, to anyone who would listen, of the importance of examples set by the adults, teachers, older children, explaining that children, in the old saying, *do what we do, not what we say.*

Here is an example of modeling as well as peer teaching. One evening after dinner I asked the music teacher, who was meeting with older students, for a lesson on the school's traditional Tibetan-Nepali stringed instrument called the *tungna*.

Then I gave lessons on the guitar. Finally I asked each of my guitar students to teach two others.

### The Results of Our Work Together

The following was sent to me by email by Shirley Blair much later:

*Your visit legitimized the notion of child-centered education at the school, which had hitherto subscribed to rote memorization, top-down, adult-dominated, competitive, 'chalk and talk' 'learning'. Until you came, my input was a lonely voice calling in the wilderness. Many children were unhappy and felt unsuccessful. Your input from an education authority, recognized worldwide helped to 'unpin' us from the old model.*

*Among other things: Slowly but surely, SMD became a happier place. Here are some examples:*

*1.* Best effort *award was included in the term and annual award ceremonies. But grades, including final results were classified confidential, a matter for the children and their teachers (and if possible, their parents - but parents are illiterate). On occasion, the student's foreign sponsors may have been included.*

*2. Ranking announcements of the top three students were discontinued.*

*3. Failures were no longer announced at term/annual award ceremonies.*

*4. Positive discipline now leads children to autonomy and good behavior by helping them understand that they are part of the school family, that we are all connected, and that actions have results. Now we try to help the children to locate control within their own heart and minds.*

*5. Teachers are encouraged to implement more 'hands on' learning opportunities.*

*6. Our teachers of the younger students understood the value of this, and were able to implement it, long before the teachers of the older students, so they set the template for change and helped the other teachers.*

*This was quite an accomplishment because the teachers of younger students are women so accorded lower status in Nepali society, whereas the teachers of the older students are mainly men and high caste and unwilling to change their methods.*

*7. We started a literacy program for our support staff, the older students being the teachers. Everyone learned, at the least, how to sign his or her own name. This project helped to bring the school family close together.*

She continued:

*Our children became happier.*

*Among the teachers who segued into our new Montessori child-centered school one came to me so happy, announcing, "Shirley, I've found the joy in teaching!"*

*One day we had a team of 8 - 9 pediatricians visiting from Scandinavia and Germany. They stayed for three hours. The next day, the head doctor asked if they could come back. "Why?" I wondered out loud.*

*"We didn't see any aggression" was the answer. They had argued about it on the way back to the teaching hospital and wanted to come again to check their perceptions. Upon their return they observed two hours on a busy, crowded playground. There was no aggression and they saw many*

117

*children helping and teaching others, of kids teaching others...*

*Academics improved and students remember what they learn. Now we encourage the children to go into two fields: education and health care. So far we have trained eleven health assistants (requiring three years intensive training abroad) as paramedic cum barefoot doctors, exactly what is needed in the mountains. We've also been training teachers - encouraging them to get undergraduate degrees (a prerequisite for teaching in Nepal).*

A 2021 Update: Because of the Pandemic all of the students have returned to their villages because they are safer from the pandemic. In some villages there is Internet so they have offered online classes.

Also the older students have created "schools" for the younger students in their villages. There are sixteen of these physical classes. They try to use Montessori principles all the way.

# TIBET, Braille without Borders (BWB)

## Kathmandu to Lhasa

There were four of us — driver, guide, and four Americans — traveling overland from Kathmandu to Lhasa. The windstorm came to us without warning. I hid my face inside my coat and tried to breathe slowly and not panic. There was no way to know how long, how large, just be calm. The driver had no choice but to keep driving but since we were not on a road, just the open high level plains of Tibet, at least there was no worry about going off the road. Finally we were through it. This experience and that of the cold, the road cut through 15 feet of snow, getting stuck crossing a stream and sitting for hours waiting for help, the freezing mountain passes and the strong winds, all made me think over and over about what it must have been for the refugee children making this trip, hiding and hoping for food and sometimes a ride, taking twenty or more days on foot.

In a tiny building — a home at night, and a restaurant during the day — we stopped for Tibetan yak milk tea and food. The room was richly decorated with beautiful Tibetan colors and images on the walls and ceiling. A young child and an infant were sound asleep on one of several benches covered with Tibetan rugs along three walls. There were three small tables and an old stove in the middle room warmed us. The room was filled with pilgrims and other Tibetans in warm but ragged clothing. Looking at the menu we saw the words "oxygen - large or small" and at first thought it was a mistranslation of a word from Tibetan to English. It was not. It was indeed oxygen. The guide told us it was necessary so we purchased one for each of us and one probably saved the life of one of us.

The scenes on these highest planes on the planet presented a unique beauty. We saw the most brilliant blue of pure clean sky one can imagine, mountains of rust, reds, blues, and browns. The only plants were a dark red-brown low brush, and sometimes fields of low growing dark green vegetation feeding herds of sheep and black yaks. As the sun rose and set, the shades of blue were even more beautiful in contrast to the red-orange-yellow edges of the clouds.

Why had I come? In 2002 I had been in Dharamsala, India studying Tibetan Buddhism and sharing Montessori information with the teachers at The Tibetan Children's Village. Upon returning home I was often asked about the reasons Tibetans leave their home and come to Nepal and India. I wanted to see for myself.

### The Tibetan Children's Villages, India

Here I must backtrack one year. In visiting the Montessori classes in two Tibetan settlements in Northern India I was very pleased at what I found. The word "Montessori" is not protected by copyright and can be used, and is used, by anyone for any purpose. There are Montessori schools, books, and materials, that often have very little to do with authentic Montessori practice and I am quite used to visiting schools like this and helping however possible. So it was such a treat to find real Montessori classes in the foothills of the Himalayas.

I discovered that the main reason was because the training of the Montessori teachers here began with "Abs" Joosten. Let me tell you a little bit about him. Albert Joosten (1914–1980) attended Montessori schools in Holland and as an adult was one of Montessori's earliest students. When Montessori and her son went to India in 1947, Mr. Joosten joined her in this work. Two years later he became the Director of the Indian Montessori Training Courses. In the 1960s it was decided that the Montessori system of education would be the best for the arriving Tibetan refugee children. Mr. Joosten and two Indian Montessori teachers began the training of teachers in 1970. (In 1977, three years before he died, Mr. Joosten was my oral examiner at the end of my 6-12 training in Washington, DC).

One of their students, Ngawang Sherab, eventually became the main teacher trainer and, by the time I met him in 2002, he had trained teachers for nine years. He gave me a copy of the TCV (Tibetan Children's Village) Montessori Curriculum published in Tibetan and English. What I saw in the classes and in this publication reassured me that Montessori was in good hands in the Tibetan refugee settlements.

Here are examples from the training manual:

*The class* would consist of one teacher and one assistant for 30-34 children from age three to six. The teachers learned to give one-to-one lessons following a child's stage of development and interests, free choice of work and uninterrupted concentration, and extensive observation and record keeping. At the end of the day the classroom would be checked to see that everything was clean and in order, often with teacher and students working together.

*The Culture lessons* were complete — physics, biology, history, arts, and music.

*The practical life activities were complete and reflected the Tibetan culture.* Examples: "how to carry a chawkyi" (a small wooden stool used as a table while the child sits on the floor), "how to wash and cut different vegetables and fruits", "how to make *momos* (small Tibetan dumplings) and butter tea", "how to put Tibetan tassels in the hair", "how to yawn and sneeze in public", "how to apologize", "how to express refusal of a further helping (of food) or to ask for a further helping", "how to help people in need", "how to receive a guest and offer a cup of tea", "how to make the offering of seven water bowls (at home or in class)" and much more.

*The sensorial, language, math, and geometry* areas were complete

## BRAILLE WITHOUT BORDERS, THE SCHOOL

Just before leaving for Tibet my husband Jim had shown me an article in The New York Times about a school for blind children in Lhasa called *Braille without Borders*. It had been created by a blind woman from Germany, Sabriye Tenberken, and run by her and Paul Kronenberg from Holland. The article was about her book, recently translated into English from German, called, *My Path Leads to Tibet*. Sabriye, who became blind as a teenager, continued her education through university and then applied to the German Peace Corps. Her application was rejected so she funded her own trip to Tibet and traveled alone on horseback looking for blind children to help.

I contacted the school and made arrangements to visit. At university she had majored in Central Asian Studies, and in addition to Mongolian and Chinese languages she wanted to study Tibetan but there was no Tibetan Braille system, so by 1992 Sabriye had developed Tibetan Braille, which later became the official reading and writing system for the blind in Tibet.

One of the students, a young blind Tibetan girl named Kyila, gave my three traveling companions and me a tour of the school. I would like to share her story.

*I was born in 1984 near Mount Everest. In my family there are six people – my parents, two brothers my older sister and I. My life was very difficult because my two brothers, my father and I are blind. My mother had to take care of us all. Being blind in Tibet is really difficult because people think of blindness as a punishment for doing something wrong in a past life. We could never go out and play with other children. My parents wanted to do everything for us and would not let us do things for ourselves. I sometimes felt that we were not only blind but also physically handicapped. It was not only the four of us who faced these challenges but most of the blind people in Tibet.*

*When I was twelve I went to a school called Braille Without Borders, the first blind school in Tibet. At that time I did not know how to dress or wash myself. I only spoke my mother tongue, which is Tibetan and had no previous education. On my first day at school I was a bit nervous and very excited. I met lots of students who were also blind. It felt as though I was in heaven, to be amongst children my own age who had had the same experiences as me.*

*I had always believed that I was totally different from sighted people. Fortunately this is not true. Although I am blind, I am not stupid and can do everything that sighted people can do. This was a revelation to me; I was seeing a new world. I felt free and full of energy.*

*The first things I learned were how to dress myself, how to make my own bed, how to eat by myself and how to wash myself. After that I learned Chinese, English, computer and orientation skills and Braille. In the first three years I learned all these things.*

After the tour around the school I gave Kyila some of my warm clothing, a little money, and the Montessori teaching manual I had brought from Dharamsala.

## Kyikyi's School

Years later I heard from Sabriye and Paul that this visit changed Kyila's life. She started her own preschool, called Kyikyi (happy) Kids, using Montessori principles inspired by the Tibetan Children's Village Montessori training manual. Her school, near Lhasa, was the first integrated kindergarten in China. Blind Tibetan children lived and studied along with young children who had been left orphans after the earthquake in 2008. Here is the motto of BWB and now of her school:

*Empower the blind before they become dis-abled.*

### Montessori at Kyila's School

Just as the first *casa dei bambini* in Rome was created out of necessity, this school was created out of necessity and as a result of it being integrated—blind and sighted children together—there were many discoveries made. For example the gap between blind and sighted children in the daily life began to close.

#### Practical Life

There were small child-sized toilets, low door handles; everything was designed to support independence of the small children. For Montessori *practical life*, called *daily life skills*, all of the children were taught the proper ways to dress themselves, feed and wash themselves, to cut vegetables, to tie shoes and use scissors, and to care for the garden and small animals at the school, and to take care of the school and help each other.

#### Movement

For large and small movement development, the use of the small white cane was taught right away for the blind children to aid their movement and independence, but the sighted children also learned to close their eyes and use the cane, making them more aware not only of their own movement, and the environment, but how it feels to be blind. The children learned to be confident in swimming, running, riding bikes, dancing, playing ball, and climbing trees. All of the children developed fine motor skills through gardening and cooking and their regular schoolwork.

*Education of the Senses*

The sense of touch was refined through matching fabrics. The walls of the school were bright and there was lovely art and bright colors. For the blind children the art on the wall was three dimensional, again making use of different materials and fabrics, again enriching the world of art for both the blind and sighted children. When playing ball a bell attached to the ball taught the children to listen carefully to judge the distance and place of the ball. Music was an important element.

*Reading and Writing and Math*

Print materials for learning reading and writing and math — in English, Tibetan, and Chinese — were available for the sighted children. In the school for the blind Sabriye had invented sensorial braille letters very much like the Montessori sandpaper letters. Each letter was a wooden board with fingernail size Braille dots cut out of felt and glued onto the board in the appropriate Braille 6-dot pattern.

The blind children learned the alphabet by touch, and unexpectedly the sighted children learned their letters very quickly using the Braille materials! Both of the groups of children, just as in any Montessori class, learned to read before the age of five.

Recently Sabriye told me:

*When I visited her kindergarten [preschool] I was surprised to see that these little kids of three and four were reading the regular Braille on paper. And they were writing Braille with stylus and slate. This is not easy at all, because you have to think in mirror writing. Later they used a Braille typewriter that is much faster.*

At age six, these children were ready to join the BWB preparatory classes for one year of intensive preparation and then integrate into mainstream Chinese schools. Between 2011 and 2016 Kyikyi had more than 30 graduates who were attending regular schools all in different levels. In fact, the stories of all of the graduates of BWB exhibit much of the philosophy of Montessori — the love of work, independence in acting and thinking, carving their own unique path while thinking of others. This is very much like the *cosmic task* idea in Montessori.

Here are some stories of the blind graduates of BWB sent to me from Sabriye and Paul:

*Most of the blind graduates went on to regular schools until university. But some couldn't care less about schooling. Gyendsen for example, although he was top in his class of fifty sighted children, he had 100% in English, math, and Tibetan and 85%, in Chinese but he was so bored that he felt he wouldn't learn anything more of value there. He came back to BWB and studied computers, first on his own, then later in Japan and Malaysia. After his training at Kanthari (see below about this project) in 2009, he* started with the Braille-book production. He produced Braille books for the students in regular schools in Chinese, English, and Tibetan. He organized a team of sighted persons, they read and then entered them into a computer. With the help of a Braille printer, he now prints them in Braille and ships them to boarding schools.

Nyima Chokpa went through BWB and the Chinese schools, and then studied journalism in Chengdu. She is a good writer and a poet, writing beautiful Tibetan poems. The state school for disabled children employed her later as a teacher. They had taken in our blind kids but realized that they didn't really know how to empower the blind.

Norbu dropped out of regular school, just like Gyendsen, because he was bored. Instead he became interested in making cheese. He received an offer to go to Holland to learn how to make cheese and, upon returning to BWB, ran a cheese factory at our training farm. He made very delicious Lhasarella (a bit like a Brie) and Tibetino (a bit like Parmesan). Later he started his own restaurant, and in 2017 was still making cheese and also supplying local Tibetan products.

Tashi Pünzog went through school and became a musician. Together with other graduates, Tashi sings and performs rock music and Tibetan traditional music, traveling all over China. The founder of his music group is Dachung who dropped out of regular school and started a massage clinic. Later he invested in a restaurant and worked as head of the band. Dachung is one of the graduates who *never forgets about the younger students. Every summer he organizes tutorials for them so they get a head start for the next year.*

*Bungzo, you might know her from the movie Blindsight, studied law. And Tenzin, also in Blindsight, became entrepreneur of the year for Tibet in 2013. He runs the biggest medical massage clinic in Tibet, and has about 23 colleagues, most of them blind.*

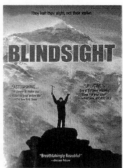

### The Movie Blindsight

Erik Weihenmayer is a famous American mountain climber who began to go blind at age fourteen and began learning to rock climb. He became world famous in 2001 as the first blind person to reach the summit of Mount Everest, the tallest mountain in the world.

Inspired by his journey Sabriye invited him to visit the school. But Erik wanted to do more. He brought six members of his climbing crew and together taught the students the basic skills of rock climbing, bonding, the essential building of trust in each other necessary for such a climb. The movie *Blindsight*, released in 2006, is a good introduction to BWB. It documents the lives before

BWB of several of the children, and it follows Erik, along with six of the BWB teenagers and their teachers, as they climb higher, both physically and emotionally, than anyone would have thought possible.

### Both Schools Close

During 2017, when many non-government organizations in China were closed, so were BWB and Kyikyi Kids kindergarten, but the lessons learned remain strong. This was heartbreaking for many, but not to be deterred, the students are studying in regular schools and the graduates are continuing their important work, often as volunteers. Kyila is presently writing a book about her life that will certainly be an inspiration for many.

### Project KANTHARI, the Work Continues in India

Several years before the schools were closed, Sabriye and Paul had expanded the work to a new project, in Kerala, India. The purpose of *Kanthari*, is to help marginalized people, including those with disabilities such as blindness, realize their dreams to drive social change in their communities. Some of the students come from as far away as countries in Africa. Kyila had spent a year taking this training in India before opening her own school in Tibet. She learned project planning, fundraising, public speaking, branding, strategies to overcome barriers to change, finances, as everything at the center is planned around each individual student and their unique passion and needs.

Sabriye has been nominated for the Nobel Peace Prize. As of 2016 there is an award-winning documentary *KANTHARI – Change from Within*. As of this writing it is free online and to watch. It tells the stories of leaders who have been affected by social ills and because of that, have taken it up to start initiatives to create a positive difference in their communities. They create a *Change from Within*.

As I communicate with Sabriye and Paul today about their project, it seems very much along the lines of what Dr. Montessori would wish, and the Montessori principles are obvious. As she says in the book *To Educate the Human Potential*:

> *The task of teaching becomes easy, since we do not need to choose what we shall teach, but should place all before [the child or young adult] for the satisfaction of his mental appetite. He must have absolute freedom of choice, and then . . . repeated experiences which will become increasingly marked by interest and serious attention, during the acquisition of some desired knowledge.*

And in the words of the famous blind mountain climber Erik Weihenmayer who inspired these children in Tibet:

> *I think this is the best time in history, the most precious time in history to be a pioneer, to reach out, to seize hold of adversity and challenges we face, to harness energy not only to transform our own lives but to elevate the world around us.*

# Montessori Teachers with the Dalai Lama in the Himalayan Kingdom of Sikkim

### San Francisco to Sikkim

On December 13, 2010, I traveled from home in Trinidad, California to San Francisco; then Dubai, UAE; then Delhi, India; then Bagdogra, India; then by car to Darjeeling, India. My friend Lhamo Pemba met me in Darjeeling and we stayed with her family. This was my first view of Kanchenjunga, the sacred mountain between Nepal and Sikkim.

A few months earlier I had received an email from my friend Adele Diamond, a neuroscientist researching executive functions of the brain in children, inviting me to join her at an education conference in Sikkim. She had thought I might already be working in Asia as I had been in Bhutan recently. I was not. She also arranged for four other Montessorians to attend.

The Sikkim government covered the costs of the four-day conference — hotel, food, and local transportation — but not international transportation for some participants. When I mentioned the opportunity to Palestinian friends with whom I had worked in the West Bank of Israel, they insisted on paying for the flight not only for me, but also for Lhamo Pemba, the first Tibetan/Bhutanese AMI teacher (now a teacher trainer). Her parents at that time were living in Darjeeling, India, not far from Bhutan, and had contacts in Sikkim.

I had never been to Northern India in the winter. There is no heating in the houses and I had spent the coldest night of my life, so covered with blankets that I could not move, before coming downstairs the first morning to get warm. I found Lhamo's mother in the family altar room praying; she took my hand and led me along with her as she carried incense into each room of the house, chanting prayer blessings. Together we had a very British breakfast of milk tea, fried egg, toast with cheese, butter and jam. We both wore coats, gloves, scarves, hats, and could see our breath as we ate breakfast.

Next she took me around the house explaining all of the family photographs and artifacts. Mrs. Pemba was born in Bhutan and her husband was born in Tibet. Dr. Pemba was the first Western-trained MD, educated in London. He was also the author of the first historical novels written about Tibet, by a Tibetan, in English. He remembered seeing the Dalai Lama arrive in Lhasa; both of them were young children then and later became friends.

Today, because Lhamo was busy, I visited the Dali Monastery next door and the classrooms of the young monks who are from 6-12 years old. I was amazed at how they managed the cold. I was wrapped in several warm layers of clothing and these young monks were running around happily outside at lunch in sandals with no socks!

For the morning I worked in the clinic helping with filing of patients' records, had rice in the monastery for lunch, and took a taxi to town to find an Internet café to catch up on email. There were twelve people in the small taxi, (twenty cents each fare) but we were prevented from coming home on time because a Muslim celebration blocked traffic for an hour. The celebration is called Hasha Hucha and remembers two brothers, sons of a king, who fought over succession and one was killed. There were loud drums and decorations and men taking turns pretending to fight to the death with wooden swords.

As the exchange rate for changing dollars to rupees was in our favor, Lhamo and I had rupees leftover after paying for our flights. We took the extra money to a nearby home for the elderly, handing out small bills to each of the old people to their great delight. After completing our paperwork and having our entry photos taken, we were driven to the border between Sikkim and the rest of India, entered, and went on to Gangtok, Sikkim for the four-day meeting.

The influence of Western culture has created many difficulties throughout the Himalayan region as well as to many developing countries: materialism, TV and computer violence, daily stress, competition replacing cooperation, isolation of the young from the elders, drugs, casual sex, negative self-image, depression and other problems.

In Sikkim, even though the government allots 20% of the budget to education, and has the highest paid teachers in India, the problem had become crucial in especially the teen-age population. One example was that seeing violence on television was leading to violence carried out by teenagers because having seen others being destructive and violent they thought it normal behavior. And the rate of depression and suicide at this age was increasing as it is in many places.

### The Conference, "Science, Spirituality, and Education"

In its wisdom, the government of Sikkim, in consultation with the Dalai Lama, had brought together a stellar group of scientists, philosophers, and educators, including six of us Montessorians, in hopes of solving these problems through the education of children, and of adults working with children.

Gangtok is a favorite tourist destination during much of the year, filled with monasteries, shrines, and temples of this ancient center of Tibetan Buddhist pilgrimage. Tibetan food is easily available. We had mostly clear blue skies revealing panoramic views of the snow-capped Mount Kanchenjunga, seen through the many strands of prayer flags. The conference was held in a large government-building auditorium, and sponsored by The Namgyal Institute of Tibetology.

The Dalai Lama opened the conference with Sikkim traditional lighting of lamps, chanting by monks, and an address. He told us of his life-long interest in science and quoted Buddha, Investigate and experiment, do not accept my teachings out of faith and devotion, as a directive to investigate everything scientifically.

There were forty speakers, including Lynne Lawrence, Executive Director of Association Montessori Internationale, Jean Miller, AMI 6-12 teacher trainer, and 80 of us observers/commenters.

An outline of the session topics:

1: Understanding our Brain

2: Understanding our Mind

3: Brain Plasticity and Mental Transformation

4: The Dalai Lama's Discussion of Moral Ethics in the Modern Education System

5: Discussion on Introducing Moral Ethics in the Modern Educational System

6: The Art and Science of Meditation Education Systems

7: Social Emotional Learning (SEL) and Education

The input on these topics by anthropologists, physicists, medical doctors in both Western and Traditional medicine, Tibetan scholars, educators, philosophy professors, psychologists, sociologists, entrepreneurs helping people in developing countries, and mindfulness researchers, was far-reaching and profound.

### Back to the Hotel

The conference days were arranged so all of the speakers and the observers could get to know each other — and participate in continual conversations — during meals, in the evenings in the hotel, and on bus rides or walks back and forth from the hotel to the conference.

I don't usually have caffeinated tea in the evening, but I didn't want to miss any of the fascinating dinner conversations so I returned to the buffet table after our meal. After requesting and being given a cup of Darjeeling tea I asked if could have a little milk. The young waiter, with the pot of tea still in his hand, stood stock still with his mouth hanging wide open. I knew he was trying to find the words to express politely what he had to say.

Finally, "But madam, this is DARJEELING tea!" I got the message and have since learned that what we call Darjeeling tea here at home is a mixture of other leaves with what might, or might not, be the pure item that only grows in the Darjeeling or Kalimpong Districts in West Bengal India.

### The Conference Continues

I admit that I have never had much patience with sitting and listening to someone talk (causing a lot of problems in school growing up), but it seems that we were all on the edge of our seats at each conference presentation, listening to every word, sorting and classifying and rearranging our brains with these new perspectives on life and human possibilities.

The Western medical doctors and Tibetan Traditional doctors had long discussions together, listened to each other and learned. The career of Tenzin Negi, PhD, clinical researcher with Emory University and NIH has focused on the potential of the mind to affect well-being on physical, emotional, and mental levels. He shared his clinical research on the behavioral, immune and stress impacts of meditation.

Richard Davidson, Ph.D. (brain researcher) shared a quote by William James that all Montessorians can relate to (from The Principles of Psychology, William James 1890, Chapter XI, Attention):

The faculty of voluntarily bringing back a wandering attention, over and over again, is the very root of judgment, character, and will. No one is compos sui [is master of oneself} if he have it not. An education which should improve this faculty would be the education par excellence. But it is easier to define this ideal than to give practical directions for bringing it about.

### The Montessori Presentations

Now it was our turn to contribute.

The Dalai Lama had arrived at the conference after speaking for five hours to 10,000 people who had come from far and near to hear him. He looked very tired. Nine people had spoken so far, essentially presenting their work to the Dalai Lama. Lynne Lawrence, General Director of AMI, Association Montessori Internationale, was the fifth to do so.

Lynne gave a brilliant introduction to Montessori in ten minutes showing lovely Montessori classroom pictures from Africa, Asia, and the West, rich and poor, emphasizing children caring for each other. She explained that the curriculum, beginning in the early years, must allow for the children to be responsible for their learning, and we must explore ways to create a social environment in which each child is able to contribute to the other and to the environment, where doing what is right is a natural consequence of daily life. Otherwise social and moral education are just subjects on the curriculum.

She ended by quoting a child. One day, after the child had worked with the small globe of the world he had turned to the teacher and said, "This is my world. Now I understand, we are all the same, we just have different names."

As Lynne had begun to speak, and to show the pictures, the Dalai Lama had looked up, sat up straight, and paid special attention. At the end of her presentation he conferred with his translator and we heard the word "Montessori" and then he said to the group, looking directly at Lynne:

> *Montessori is wonderful. Education should teach children to say, "This is my world."*

It was a proud moment for all of us representing Montessori to this very special group of people.

Dr. Jean Miller described research in Montessori elementary, age 6-12, classes where children were put in charge of their own social behavior and class rules, and given responsibility for their own education. One interesting result was the children's desire to have school be an hour longer each day because of their ownership of their education. The school was able to allow for this. She spoke at length about social and emotional learning.

From then on many of the questions, during tea breaks and lunch and back at the hotel, were directed to us, the five Montessorians.

### An Extra Day

The conference heads asked if we could stay for an additional day after the end of the conference. Of course we accepted. We met all day with the government officials at the Namgyal Institute, with several breaks for Tibetan tea (black tea with butter and salt) or British milk tea and snacks.

The questions were excellent but there was frustration when they heard how long it takes for Montessori teachers to be trained at the different levels of development, preschool through high school in order to provide authentic Montessori.

My own contribution to the discussions on the last "Montessori" day, after forty years of both meditating and teaching Montessori, was about personal observations of children engaged in deep concentration. I said that as adults we must decide to practice

142

meditation, but children enter this state of deep concentration and mindfulness naturally.

During deep concentration on age-appropriate work they become unaware of what is going on around them. They become deeply involved in whatever they are doing, and we are careful that this meditative state is not interrupted, that children be allowed to end a period of concentration according to their own intuition. When such long periods of concentration are protected children exhibit, naturally, restfulness, satisfaction, happiness, and concern and care for others.

I am sure that because of all of the interesting conversations we had with conference participants and the government on the last day, we learned a lot, and perhaps we planted a seed that will blossom to understand more the potential of human beings.

Here is a quote from the Dalai Lama's opening address that set the tone for all of us; it is very much in line with the words of Montessori:

> *I am convinced that the progress or decline of humanity rests very largely with educators and teachers, who therefore have a tremendous responsibility. If you are a teacher, try not to merely transmit knowledge, but try at the same time to awaken your students' minds to basic human qualities such as kindness, compassion, forgiveness, and understanding.*

# RUSSIA, Montessori Help
# for Severe Disabilities

In the spring of 2010, following work in Moscow I took the train to St. Petersburg to visit a Montessori school and see the beautiful architecture and the Hermitage Museum. But life is full of surprises. My friend took me to visit "Dynamics," a school for children with severe physical disabilities. This visit was the high point of the trip. Let me tell you about it.

Dynamics is a free school for children and young adults with severe disabilities. Before it was created people with these problems stayed home, as they could not walk. There was no physical therapy and they had nothing to do. Many of these children have spina bifida, which is often accompanied by mental retardation in various degrees. Twenty years before my visit a group of parents had decided to create a place where these children and young adults could get out of the house, meet others, and make friends.

There was a shallow swimming pool that these children were entering with help, while still seated in the wheelchair, for relaxing muscles and bringing smiles of happiness on the faces. I observed a dance class where everyone was encouraged to participate at some level.

There were costumes for fashion shows. The main rule was that staff members could only work at Dynamics if they really love their work, and it was clear that everyone I met fulfilled this requirement.

Three years before our visit an amazing doctor joined the staff. Dr. Natalia had received her AMI Montessori 3-6 training in Munich and had taken an additional Montessori course for working with special needs children. Upon her return she spent two years training six women. They filled a small room with tall bookcases, within reach of a person seated in a wheelchair, of Montessori materials where each of the 130 children in the school were able to spend thirty-five minutes a week with individual help on how to use the materials.

I asked if we could see a student working in the Montessori room. Pavel had been born with spina bifida and had never learned to walk, or use his hands, or speak. At age eight he had begun coming to Dynamics. But aside from the warm pool that he could enter in his new wheelchair, and the community of others and very kind adults, he had not shown any improved development, either mentally or physically. As a result no one knew anything about his intelligence or about what had been going on in his mind.

Three years ago, as soon as this program began, Pavel had been introduced to the Montessori room in his wheelchair for the first time. He was unable to move on his own, but he looked and looked at the beautiful materials on the shelf. Then he tried to move his hands for the first time, just to touch the colorful wooden materials. Imagine a person who for nineteen years had been completely taken care of and never been inspired to try to move his hands. Imagine just how difficult it must be to begin this very difficult enterprise after a lifetime. The messages sent to the brain, and from there, through the nerves to the muscles, for the first time!

Pavel, like all of the other students, began a weekly appointment schedule in the Montessori room. He was first attracted to the practical life activity of wiping a table with a cloth. I thought it very interesting that he would be attracted, not so much to the beautiful Montessori sensorial materials, but to the possibility of attempting an activity that he had seen others carry out probably almost every day of his life — wiping a table.

This preference of even the youngest children to be allowed to do the real work they have seen adults carry out is something that has been observed in Montessori environments all over the world. Such activities provide an individual the opportunity to be an active and contributing member of a social group. So we know that it is not only important physically and mentally, but also emotionally and spiritually.

Pavel had watched carefully as the adult showed him the steps of wiping the surface of a table with a cloth, and finally he tried to lift his hand and reach for the material. This was his first attempt at a whole-hand, repetitive, real work.

He grinned from ear to ear as he was wheeled into the room after I requested to see someone in the environment. Since it was at my request and not his regular time perhaps it was even a bit more exciting.

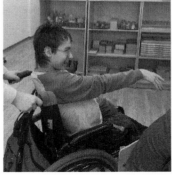

Pavel's challenge for today was to work with one of four Montessori *cylinder blocks*. The first time he had worked with this material the teacher had slowly removed each of the cylinders from the matching spaces in the large wooden block, and placed each one exactly in front of the hole where they belong. Pavel had slowly, and with great effort, learned to lift each cylinder and place it in the matching space.

What he was going to be shown on this day was more physically challenging. Dr. Natalia removed the cylinders, but this time she mixed them up on the table. This would require both mental and physical effort. Pavel would have to grasp the knob, lift, and move the cylinder along the block, along all of the empty spaces until he found the correct one, and lower it to fit the cylinders into the correct space.

It took a long time because this required a lot of moving, but when Pavel had finished replacing each cylinder the glowing smile on his face was that of someone who had just won the Nobel Peace Prize, or the lottery.

What Pavel had accomplished in the Montessori room with Dr. Natalia was a miracle. It was because of this experience, and his mastering of a special computer keyboard requiring minimum movement, that his high intelligence revealed itself.

Although he was still developing more and more of the control of his hands, he had learned to use many of the materials and to communicate his thoughts and to do research on a computer. He had learned to do research on the Internet and with this very limited movement had excelled in several academic subjects.

When we asked what would happen to Pavel now that he is too old to continue with the school faces dropped. There was no place for him to continue to learn in this way, but he knows about the theoretical physicist and cosmologist Stephen Hawking who as a young adult had developed a motor neural disease, but continued his work in the same way that Pavel was now working. This gives him a goal for going forward.

# MOROCCO, an Orphanage, Village Schools, and a Garden

Whenever I am working in a new country I want to learn as much as I can about the families and children in that country.

During my first trip to Morocco in 2015 my hostess and her family and I were able to accompany a group of medical people far out into the desert of Taroudant to visit a *madrasa* (the Arabic word for traditional school) where the eye doctors and staff would examine and treat the eyes of the elementary and high school students. We were able to see how the students lived and studied.

At one point, being asked why we had come, my friend Aicha, head of the Montessori school in Casablanca, showed the teachers a short video clip of one of the primary classes at her school on her phone. Being used to the traditional methods of education they were amazed at the calmness, children moving about freely involved in independent purposeful activity.

But I also wanted to see the lives of the very young so upon our return to Casablanca we arranged to visit an orphanage where infants and very young children were cared for.

Here is a quote about that visit from my book *Montessori and Mindfulness*:

> *I visited an orphanage in Casablanca where there was an interest in Montessori, but there were no trained people or materials. Children under the*

age of one spent most of the day lying on a slanted mattress in a crib because there were not enough staff to sufficiently burp the babies after being fed. When they were a little older the infants spent some time in swings and walkers – objects that we in the Montessori field know not to use.

After thinking about everything I saw, I suggested to the owner of the Montessori school, who wanted to do something to help the orphanage, that they develop a First Year Montessori Project. In the first year of life a lot of vital developmental support can be provided with little training and materials, compared to age one and older.

Over the next year teachers at Ecole Montessori Casablanca volunteered to visit the orphanage, to make materials, and to create a Montessori environment for the first year.

When I returned to Morocco the following year the changes at the orphanage were dramatic. I met with the staff and the pediatrician connected with the orphanage to share more about Montessori and to hear their stories. They had had no idea that children

150

*this young could move, explore the environment, exhibit curiosity, and concentrate as they had now seen. Nor had they imagined that there could be this level of independence. I heard this comment, "Their eyes are different. It is as though their eyes are open for the first time."*

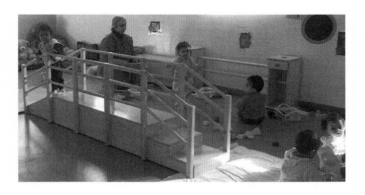

### From the 2018 annual report
### of the AMI affiliate for Morocco:

*This year has marked an important stride in our outreach work. Association Montessori Morocco has offered the AMI assistant training to staff members of the orphanage we are partnered with. They left the training full of energy and ambition to revolutionize the orphanage environment and incorporate as much practical life as possible. Association Montessori Morocco has donated some materials in support of their work and efforts, and continues to offer in house visits and trainings. We have offered AMI training to their staff members. We are also partnering with another orphanage who are interested in implementing Montessori principles within their primary and elementary environments.*

A few years later I was able to share this experience, the potential for valuable help with just a few changes, in South America. *Colegio Bilingue Montessori* in Cali, Colombia has for years been involved with many humanitarian projects, including working with the staff at a nearby orphanage.

Lyda Franky, the head of the school, and I visited the orphanage. We shared as much Montessori infant and early childhood information as we could in one visit and gave them a copy of my book used in Morocco, *The Joyful Child: Montessori, Global Wisdom for Birth to Three*, but they wanted it translated.

As a result Lyda, and other volunteers from Colombia, Peru, Mexico, Morocco, Paraguay, and even northern Morocco, have translated it. Here is the title in Spanish: *EL Niño Alegre: Montessori desde el Nacimiento hasta los Tres Años*.

### Help for Moroccan Village Schools

Rita El Kadiri, a parent at Ecole Montessori Casablanca, was at the time of my visit to Morocco in 2016, CEO of the Foundation Zakoura, whose aim is to create schools for the poor village children of Morocco. Since her daughter began attending the Montessori school in Casablanca she had become interested in figuring out how to share Montessori practices in these village schools.

Rita, Aicha, and Leila from the school, and I spent a morning observing and visiting the children and teachers at the project school in El Jadida south of Casablanca. The classrooms were sparse and small, children studying in the traditional ways, listening to the teacher and using worksheets. But because of the interests of one of the staff members there was a beautiful garden at this school with not only local plants, but also a collection of plants from many countries, all clearly labeled for the children to learn about.

In the afternoon we had a very long and fruitful discussion. We wanted to figure out ways to incorporate the cultural values of Morocco, while gradually moving toward giving the children more general knowledge and independence.

At the end of the week we met again, this time also with Rita's head teachers with the village project and I presented a paper of ideas. I shared my experience of teaching a class of children the same age in Lima, Peru with no Montessori materials. Next I suggested widening the subject of the worksheets to include local cultural examples of Morocco. Aicha and I talked about the value of practical life and involving the children more in the care of the school, the classroom, and the outside environment. And because of the example of the wonderful garden at the school we had visited I suggested cooperation with gardeners, farmers, others involved in the everyday life of each village where there was to be a new small school.

As a result of our work over 100 small village schools throughout Morocco have been improved and Rita wrote to me later, "Your visit was enlightening and we developed a whole curriculum inspired by Montessori."

### From Headstart Programs in Oakland California to Morocco – A Garden Fieldtrip for the Students of the First AMI 3-6 Teacher Training Course

*Headstart* is a preschool program, begun in 1965. It helps young children from low-income families do well in elementary school by fostering children's growth in social, emotional, cognitive, and physical development. In the 1980s I was asked to help in California with Montessori ideas, to share activities and lessons teachers could give that reflected the focus of Montessori schools.

It was clear that there was no chance of there being, at this stage, Montessori teacher training or materials but there was a lot that could be done, by introducing the basic Montessori primary class "cultural" lessons in physics, biology, geography, history, art, and music. This is the way we "bring the world into the classroom."

A Montessori primary class teacher begins with these lessons; the practical life exercises give the children tools for caring for everything in the cultural areas of the classroom; the sensorial materials sharpen their perceptions to explore them; and the language—speaking, writing and reading—are enriched by the exposure to the whole world in this way.

Even in homes, and in preschools not at all practicing Montessori, these activities can enrich the early life of children.

For the first *Headstart* talk I decided to begin with physics. The meeting with the teachers from many public schools in the poorest areas of Oakland was scheduled. I went to the local Montessori school to see if I could borrow the 3-6 class physics materials on a Friday afternoon after school to use on the weekend. I was surprised to find out that there were none!

In talking to the teacher I discovered that the culture lessons given in my training in London are not part of all training courses. I gathered the material as best I could, and inspired a group of teachers with simple ways of introducing the concepts of electricity, magnetism, air and water, sound, and light.

Since then I have given these and other culture lectures and workshops in places as varied as New Zealand and the Ural Mountains of Russia.

In 2019 I gave them at the first AMI 3-6 course to be given in Morocco.

*Physics*

The culture lectures on the course began with physics. Simple sink and float, exploring air and water, sound, electricity, heat, light. As is always the case in Montessori teacher training courses, the students spent a lot of time with the materials, giving lessons to each other to discover the many ways children might respond to such lessons. The teachers-in-training clearly enjoyed exploring physics just as much as children do.

*Botany*

Here are some of my notes from one of the botany lectures presented to the teachers-in-training:

*We began by looking at a PowerPoint with pictures of the many botanical concepts such as parts of the leaf, leaf to stem attachment, parts of the stem, simple and compound leaves, leaf vein systems, the variety of margins, leaf shapes — all elements that*

*they would find in nature after the presentations.*
*Then together we went on a nature walk in a*
*beautiful garden in the home of my hosts.*

*The students were hesitant at first, but very*
*quickly found themselves as excited as children as*
*they discovered the ways that the leaves were*
*attached to the stems — alternately, oppositely, or*
*whorled, a group of leaves all attached at the same*
*point. I could see them crouched down looking close*
*to the ground excitedly discovering a leaf shape they*
*were looking for in the tiniest of tiny garden weeds.*
    *Upon discovering a leaf with a combination of*
*parallel veins and dentate margins (which is very*
*rare) one student called to the others, "Come and see*
*what I found!" I overheard an interesting discussion*
*about the fact that there were more than one leaf*
*shape on the* sansevieria *plant and on the fig tree —*
*so the label didn't depend on the name of the plant*
*but on the shape of the leaf.*
    *This is the point I wanted them to discover*
*because when children are looking for shapes they*

*can find them and name them without any*
*knowledge of the local name of the plant.*

*This is an important step in independent*
*research, allowing even the young child to identify,*
*classify, and name with no need for help from an*
*adult.*

*As we prepared to leave the garden and headed*
*down the path toward the vehicles, I noticed several*
*of the students walking extremely slowly toward the*
*exit of the garden, looking carefully and closely at*
*plants, taking pictures with their phones, some*
*leaving the garden with great reluctance. This is just*
*the kind of involvement we will see in children and it*
*is helpful for us adults to know what this feels like.*

**Note:** The year after this teacher-training course I published these lectures in the book *The Red Corolla, Montessori Cosmic Education* (for age 3-6) that is being used by parents and teachers.

*Cosmic education* is the basic structure of all Montessori education. In the early years children discover and experience the world through their senses in ways described here. After that the emphasis is on discovering the interrelatedness of all elements of the universe and discovering one's own meaningful role.

This work with the students who were studying to become Montessori teachers in Morocco began in California. This is an example of the concept of *planting seeds*; one can never know where, and when, the little seeds we plant will sprout and grow and spread.

# THAILAND, Educateurs sans Frontières (ESF)

Maria Montessori once said that since there is a Red Cross organization for physical health emergencies, there should also be another organization, called the White Cross, which would respond to emergencies to help children in traumatic situations. Such a project was not created during her lifetime but her youngest granddaughter, Renilde Montessori, revitalized this idea in 1999, and named it Educateurs san Frontières.

She said, "When using the term Educateurs sans Frontières, we refer to borders that transcend the obvious ones to do with nation states. The truly important ones are the psychological and spiritual frontiers the ideological, religious, racial, social and economic, cultural and linguistic boundaries which artificially divide a humanity as yet largely unaware of its intrinsic unity and interconnectedness with the earth that brought it forth."

Ours was the fourth EsF assembly, held in August 2015 over two weeks in Khon Kaen, Thailand. There were sixty-six participants from twenty-six countries. We were there to share, or to learn about and discuss, innovative solutions for social change, and how to use Montessori principles to reach our goals. Many of the participants had very little experience with Montessori so their insight combined with the experience of those of us who had been teaching for a long time was rich and productive for all.

Together we visited the Montessori school in the community, and over the weekend broke into groups to go on field trips. I spent that day exploring an archeological dig and museum with several young teachers from China. Our conversations during the long trip in the van were as interesting as the rest of the field trip. There were many bonds formed, between people from many countries, during this assembly.

I am going to share two of the many projects from this meeting.

### Born Inside, Babies Born in Prison

Years ago Beverley Maragh, Montessori teacher-trainer in London, was disturbed by the many babies born in prison and wanted something to help the situation. Lynne Lawrence, general director or the Association Montessori Internationale (AMI), encouraged Beverley to visit a prison and see what could be done. So Beverley began to create a way to help. Along with a friend psychotherapist she assists mothers and babies in prison. The project is known as Born Inside.

Their work began at a prison situated in North London, in January 2012, and then spread to a second prison. They visit each prison one day a week, spending one hour with the mothers and babies on the mother and baby unit. Then they spend an additional hour with the pregnant women, seeing each person individually.

*UK statistics shared with us:*

Annually, approximately 17, 240 children are separated from their mothers. Fathers care for only 9% of these children. 15% of these women are foreign nationals. 46% of the women have experienced domestic violence. 53% of the women have experienced emotional, physical and sexual abuse as children. 66% of women in prison have dependent children under the age of 18 years. Around one-third of women prisoners lose their homes, and often their possessions, while in prison. A Prisons Inspectorate survey found that 38% of women in prison do not have accommodation arranged on release.

In one of the two prisons, as an example, there are approximately five hundred women. On this mother and baby unit there is space for twelve mothers and thirteen babies, one of the rooms is reserved for twins. The mothers must apply for a space and then present themselves to a board that will make the decision whether or not to offer them a place on the unit. The babies can stay until they are 18 months old.

The women that Beverley and her colleague have worked with are 18 to 42 years old. About 25% of the women they have worked with have husbands or fathers who are also in prison. Some of the women were first time mothers and for some this was their ninth child, and a couple of the women were even grandmothers themselves. Sometimes they have worked with three generations at one time (grandmother, mother, daughter).

*Examples of how they have helped with the Montessori approach:*

1 – They share information about the importance of movement in early childhood development.

2 – The mothers are encouraged to lay their babies on their tummies when they are awake and to allow the child space to move on the floor.

3 – Mothers are shown simple toys, that can be made, and that are small enough for a baby's hand.

4 – Together they look at and discuss clothing that allows movement. And the importance of not putting babies into shoes unless they are walking.

5 – They encourage mothers to talk directly to their babies and to use correct pronunciation of their words. They explain the importance of a mother to speak in her native language first.

6 – Mothers are taught the importance of reading to the babies and cutting down on television time.

*Achievements that Beverley shared:*

The mothers began to set up the room before it was time for the session. They began to sit on the floor with their babies, and started to actively play and enjoy the achievement of their own children. Mothers started to collaborate in planning and cooking meals for the babies. This was all possible while they are in prison.

When mothers were released, some of the mothers continued to connect with Beverley and her colleague outside of the prison and to share in their child's developmental progress. They began to express their hopes for themselves and their babies since being released from prison.

By the time Beverley shared this project with us in 1995, Born Inside had been operating for four and a half years, helping over sixty mother and baby pairs, and forty-five babies from five days of age to fifteen months. They were at this time, in 1995, also working with over one hundred pregnant mothers in prison.

They have continued this work until now, temporarily halted because of the Covid-19 epidemic. What an inspiration this work is for all of us.

## *Montessori for the Elderly and Forgetful*

The other project concerned help for the elderly, including those living with dementia. Before I share that, here is a story of my own experience that led me to want to know more about this work.

One year I was visiting the home of parents of a dear friend. The mother of my friend was suffering from Alzheimer's and she could do nothing to care for herself; everything was taken care of by the loving people around her. She was standing near me as I washed the dishes, watching my hands carefully. It reminded me of a typical situation with a young child. Slowly I moved the dish cloth to the counter next to the sink, next to her, smoothed it out, and went through the stages of folding the cloth, first in half and then in fourths, holding the corners precisely in such a way that she could see clearly everything I was doing, and making each movement slow and careful.

Her eyes lit up and she looked up at me with a slightly confused smile. I asked if she would like to fold the cloth. She probably had no idea what my words meant but the meaning was clear. So again I spread the cloth out on the counter and smoothed it. She attempted to imitate me precisely just as would a child. When she finished I picked the cloth up and then smoothed it on the counter a second time, and again she attempted to fold it carefully. She repeated this action over and over and gradually became more and more successful. I believe this was an example of a person relearning what had been learned before. So much of this kind of information must be stored in our brains and bodies, accessible to older people if they have an environment that supports efforts. This was probably the most valuable and satisfying thing she had done in a long time and it was a precious moment for both of us.

Anne Kelly has led the Montessori world in this work. Anne was already a specialist in elder care when she discovered Montessori. She was drawn to it because it aligned so closely with what she had learned about how to be helpful. Her presentation was called "Changing the world of older people including those living with dementia" and her work is now spreading around the world.

Anne explained that the actual disability is that associated with dementia, the real physical and mental condition. But excess disability, which is so common and that we can affect, arises from the disuse of the remaining abilities. The goal is the prevention of excess disability.

Dementia is a term that actually describes a large group of illnesses that cause progressive decline in a person's abilities, loss of memory, rationality, social skills, and physical functioning. There are forty-four million people in the world living with dementia and it is projected that there might be 135 million by 2050. Anne said, "If dementia were a country it would be the world's 18th largest country."

Montessori can prevent excess disability in many ways. Meaningful activities and environmental supports give the person practice in using the skills that otherwise would be lost. A person can get better by practicing certain skills even if they do not remember ever having had such skills and a person can relearn skills that have been lost.

She gave examples of providing practical life work, activities that individuals had participated in throughout life, Montessori-type language materials and clues. It reminded me very much of my experience showing my friend's mother how to fold a dishcloth. It seemed to me that she was remembering something she had done many times in her life, and that brought her happiness.

Years later when talking about this experience with a friend from Japan, she told me, "Quite often boys are not expected to do the household shores such as cleaning the house, cooking, washing dishes. This is thought of as girls' work. You can see the results at "Home for the aged" now. Men don't have anything to do while women are so active and happy!"

Here is a quote from Montessori for Aging and Dementia on the AMI site: The goal of the Montessori program is to support older adults and people living with dementia by creating a prepared environment, filled with cues and memory supports, that enable individuals to care for themselves, others, and their community. We strive to develop communities that treat individuals with respect and dignity and honor their choices so that they may live as independently as possible.

*Here are some of the results Anne shared with us:* enhanced function; increased display of pleasure (smiling, laughing); enhanced conversation abilities;

decreased disruptive behaviors (wandering, repetitive questioning); decreased sleeping; improved family member or visitor satisfaction, and decreased family member's sense of frustration.

Today there is a Montessori certificate course to train people to use Montessori principles to help people who are aging, and those with dementia.

When my mother was approaching her last years I asked Anne for advice. My mother was a musician but was losing her sight. She could still play the piano but no longer could she play her large concert harp that had been important throughout her life. Anne helped me bring music and pleasure back to my mother and I have written about this in the last chapter, on the music environment throughout life, in the book *The Red Corolla, Montessori Cosmic Education.*

My talk was about some of the ways I have shared Montessori in the Himalayas, Mongolia, Morocco and Brazil; but as usual I learned much more than I taught. This meeting was one of the inspirations for this book.

# Montessori at Home, Age 0-6

Over the years I have shared, in other books, a lot of information to help parents understand their children at different stages of development. In this and the next chapter I share solutions to a few specific and universal problems and situations encountered by parents and teachers, in many countries.

It very interesting to see people on the Internet today say that they want to begin to "homeschool" their children beginning at age two or three. Then I remember a conversation I had with a young mother on an airplane trip. She was an architect as was her husband. They had full schedules of at least 40 hours a week of work in their offices. She thought they had arranged everything very well, "We have a television in every room even the baby's room, a lovely daycare situation near the house that cares for our child from 9-5 every week day, and a nanny who is available to pick her up and babysit for her evenings and on weekends."

### All Parents are Homeschooling

I was very surprised at first but now I find that this is not an isolated situation in today's modern world. So when I hear a parent say they want to begin to homeschool very young children I think sometimes that this mother or father is just expressing a desire to spend more time with their child.

To these parents I say, "Spending time with your child in the early years is perhaps the most important job you could have."

And, just as in our culture we spend many years preparing, and continuing to educate ourselves for professions, I recommend spending as much time as possible doing the same things in preparing, and continuing to educate ourselves, for the job of parenting.

## Concentration Cannot be Taught but It can be Protected

It is not uncommon for visitors to a Montessori class of very young child to be amazed at how calm and reasonable, smiling, busy concentrating, and kind, children are being. When I showed the 0-3 video of Montessori infant communities to the staff and faculty at the boarding school in Nepal, the main comment afterward was, "These are really good children."

But I knew there was nothing unique or special about the children; their behavior was a result of the environment and the teachers. Here I will quote, once again, one of the most important observations made by Montessori, very early in her career:

> *When the children had completed an absorbing bit of work, they appeared rested and deeply pleased. It almost seemed as if a road had opened up within their souls that led to all of their latent powers, revealing the better part of themselves. They exhibited a great affability to everyone, put themselves out to help others and seemed full of good will.*
>
> *— The Child in the Family*

Such concentration is common in a Montessori class because the children have been provided with the right kind of activity for the stage of development. The teacher's full time job is to create this environment, provide the correct materials, present them one at a time to each child. These are materials and activities that have been tested for many years in many countries.

Then it is the responsibility of the teacher to observe each child, changing plans when necessary based on the child's response to a lesson, and to document the results and plan the next step for each child. That is how it works in a Montessori class.

But what about in a home when parents have so many other aspects of life to balance throughout a day? Even Montessori trained adults find it extremely difficult, when they are at home with their own children, to focus on which need of the child—exploration, order, communication, concentration, self-control, work, movement—might not be being met at any particular moment.

One of the best ways for parents to begin is to watch for children's emerging periods of concentration, to decide if it is a healthy and safe activity, and then try to avoid interrupting till the child is finished.

Shelves of appropriate toys are a very nice part of the home environment, but many parents set this up but become frustrated because the children do not play with them. This is very common!

If we think about it, children at this age are closely watching everything the children and adults in their environment, at home or at school, are doing. They want to learn to do what they see. When they see several other children working with a piece of material in school they naturally are attracted to it. They want to imitate. So what do they see in the home?

Even the very young child who is not yet walking, thrives when able to move about freely in a SAFE environment, to explore and to touch everything in sight, carpet fringe, safe pots and pans kept on a low shelf in the kitchen, items that they have seen others touch and use.

### Putting Toys Away

As far as the lovely shelves with appropriate toys, if children see someone else in the family actually playing with some of the toys that have been put out for them, they are likely to want to play with them too.

If the parent wants to teach a child to put toys away it is not a good example to rush around, moving quickly, with perhaps a frustrated look on the face, while cleaning up. But if once a day or so a parent sits down on the floor in front of the toy shelves, smiles, and slowly —

with a sincere show of careful movement and enjoyment—places the toys where they belong on the shelf, a child is far more likely to want to do the same.

One day I was helping my grandson clean leaves and fallen twigs from the sandbox. There were several trucks and cars on the sand, so I carefully lined them up on the edge of the sandbox. The next week, talking to my daughter on the phone, I learned that he had started lining up the trucks and cars neatly and spending a long time doing this, and she didn't know where this new game came from until I told her. It was a lesson for us both that he was watching carefully; we never know when our actions are going to be imitated.

### Children Want to Be Helpful

It is not easy for many parents to figure out how to include a child in the work of the home, but the beginnings can be very simple. Putting just the spoons in the dishwasher when the parent is loading the dishwasher (I watched my grandchild do that with great satisfaction), wiping the leaves of a houseplant with a tiny piece of sponge, carrying a few pieces of fruit into the house when the parent returns from shopping for groceries, slicing just one banana and arranging it on a plate to share with the family.

The examples depend completely on each family. But start small and you will be surprised.

We hand wash a lot of our laundry and during one visit my granddaughter asked if she could do her own laundry. Together we stretched a "clothesline" from the deck pole to a chair, filled a bucket with soap and warm water, and she was delighted to wash her own clothing, hang it out in the sun to dry, fold and put it away, and then roll up the clothesline and put them away with the clothespins for another day.

What if the needs of a child, for order and work and so forth, are not met at a particular time and this child explodes in loud frustration. Most parents are not able to drop everything and respond to an unhappy child immediately, especially in the common situation of one parent being home alone all day with a child, with no one to consult with except others in the same situation.

I don't mean to glorify the historical extended families because it is clear that kind of life was, or is, not perfect. But there are some things that made raising a child easier. There were many adults nearby to help with a young child, and there were elders to consult when a new parent didn't know what to do. There is a lot of what we call practical life work going on and children are gradually able to imitate and join in. Life was less confusing when the rules, the limits of behavior, were consistent.

I thought about an example that occurred many years ago. I was walking down a street in Edinburgh, Scotland. I saw two young boys drop the wrappings from some candy they were eating on the ground. An old man seated on a park bench immediately called out to the boys, even though it was clear he didn't know their names, and told them quite firmly to pick up the paper and put it in the waste container. They immediately obeyed the man, looking a little apologetic. I thought about what would happen in my country. The United States of America is a melting pot of peoples and cultures. And there are many different sets of rules or limits. It is quite often the case that the rules in one family are completely different than in another.

### Temper Tantrums

Everywhere I have worked it seems that temper tantrums are becoming a problem. In some cases a child crying "for no reason" was just not tolerated in the past and any incidence would be immediately punished. Now parents realize that it is important for children to honestly express their emotions. Temper tantrums are one of the ways young children express their emotions, unhappiness, boredom, need for attention. I hear stories from around the world that are similar:

> *Children cry or yell in order to get what they want and parents don't know what to do. When the temper tantrum happens in public they are ashamed and know that something is wrong but they don't*

*know the answer. So they give in to the child's*
*demands to end the embarrassing scene.*

Yes, in these situations we parents know that something is wrong. But what can we do about it? I will share some of what I have learned over the years.

There are emotions, expressed in temper tantrums, that are healthy and justified, and there are also those that we have trained children to exhibit.

Here is an example of the second type in my own experience. A new two-year-old girl entered my preschool Montessori classroom. I took her to the shelf, selected a knobbed puzzle, took her to a table and chair and showed her how to begin. Then I watched. She chose a puzzle piece but couldn't immediately fit the piece into one of the empty spaces. Rather than looking for another space for that puzzle piece, she threw the piece down and began to yell loudly. I showed her how to match the shape to several different empty spaces before trying to place it in the puzzle. She managed one piece, but then repeated the behavior with the second. I showed her again and she did the puzzle quickly. But each time I gave her something else to work with, and she couldn't do it perfectly immediately, she started to yell even though there was nothing anyone could do for her.

Finally, I told her that I could see she was used to yelling a lot but she should just come and get me if she really needed help. I also explained to the rest of the class that she was all right, not hurt or scared, she was just used to yelling. I would say she had about twenty temper tantrums during that first morning. The next morning she had ten tantrums; the third morning five temper tantrums; and then no more, ever. My not responding with each outburst is an example of extinguishing, rather than reinforcing, a behavior pattern, from Psychology 101.

She seemed quite relieved not to have to spend so much time yelling and trying to get someone's attention and settled very well and happily into the routine of the class.

It was such a striking change, even though the tantrums continued to a lesser degree at home, that the mother wanted to learn; so we discussed this at the next parent meeting. When observing the beginnings of temper tantrums at home I asked the parents not to change any behavior but to observe and make a note, what had happened before and what did they think the child needed, or wanted.

### Temper tantrum - Old Brain

Prevention is always more powerful than cure. The more a parent can meet the needs of a child the less chance that there will be temper tantrum. But if one occurs, it is important to understand two basic causes.

One kind of a temper tantrum, or strong negative reaction, is fully justified. It is an old brain survival reaction to an emotion such as pain, confusion, hunger, tiredness, sensory overload, missing a parent, boredom, too much TV or computer, even upsetting a sense of order, or having one's concentration interrupted!

Here are a few things to keep in mind in preparing to deal with a temper tantrum. I was reminded of them recently in a parenting talk given by a friend Heidi Philippart, an AMI Montessori 0-3 teacher trainer in Amsterdam. Her talk was broadcast throughout the world and benefitted many parents.

In the first three years of life there are three freedoms:

1 - A child needs to have freedom to move.

2 – A child needs to have freedom to communicate, to talk.

3 – A child needs to have freedom to work on something interesting.

Children in these early years cannot obey us when we are asking for something (hold still, be quiet) that goes against this life-supporting inner drive. We can help by keeping a consistent order in how the day goes so the young child knows what is coming next. And by keeping the environment simple and not chaotic, keeping things in the same place as much as possible.

Here is an example of how an upset sense of order can cause a problem.

A very young child in a neighborhood home had begun, seemingly out of the blue, to hit her father. The father, a psychologist, realized finally that his usual schedule was to leave for work every weekday morning at the same time, and on the weekend two days he would stay home. This was Christmas vacation and the third day of staying home. The sense of order of the child's life had been upset. Just an understanding of the situation defused the confusion and calmed the whole family. An infant can become very upset over things that we would not notice; for example the child, in a story told by Montessori, who cried because an umbrella, which the child had seen many times closed, was opened for the first time. A child may become disturbed as a result of being bathed after a meal when she has become accustomed to being bathed before a meal.

### Temper tantrum 2 - New Brain

The new, or higher brain, develops gradually. But just like anything else, a child needs practice in self-control. Just as there are three freedoms in Montessori 0-6 environments, there are also three limits, again, very well put during my friend's parenting talk.

1 - A child is not allowed to hurt him or her self.

2 – A child is not allowed to hurt another.

3 – A child is not allowed to be destructive to the environment.

Here is another example from personal experience. A grandson, age four was visiting for a few days. He started arguing with his older sister over something they were playing. Suddenly he started yelling, hitting her, and throwing toys. My Montessori teacher instinct immediately came into play. I gently but firmly picked him up and put him in my lap and held him firmly, even as he struggled to hit me and get away. My words were something like, "I am not angry at you. I am just holding you until you get yourself back under control, until you are back to being your wonderful self." This first time was the longest episode but he calmed down.

During a second episode we did the same thing and this took much less time. Later, at a neutral moment (when they were playing well together), I said, "If you ever feel like losing control like that you could just come and sit on the sofa next to me and see if that is all you need." This happened a few times.

Then I said, "If I am not in the room and you feel the need to control yourself, would you like to try just sitting here on the sofa to see if that helps you calm down?" It worked.

When his father came to pick up the grandchildren the first thing our grandson wanted to show him was how he could come and sit on the sofa and calm down ALL BY HIMSELF.

Setting limits clearly is in no way intended to prevent a child feeling, and expressing, emotions that are valid to the situation! These limits instead give a child a healthy way to express emotions, and a feeling of security because the child knows exactly what the limits of behavior are. So even though it is not always easy to understand what caused the first kind, we can understand that it is not purposeful, and we then decide our response either to let the child exhaust the expression alone but with us nearby, or if we need to calm the child or hold the child until it is over if the tantrum becomes violent.

Here is a quote from the book, *Whole-Brain Child*, by Daniel J. Siegel and Tina Payne Bryson that explains this in another way:

*When you know about the upstairs and downstairs brain, you can also see that there are really two different types of tantrums. An upstairs tantrum occurs when a child essentially decides to throw a fit. She makes a conscious choice to act out, to push buttons and terrorize you until she gets what she wants.*

*A parent who recognizes an upstairs tantrum is left with one clear response: never negotiate with a Terrorist. An upstairs tantrum calls for firm boundaries and a clear discussion about appropriate and inappropriate behavior.*

*A downstairs tantrum is completely different. Here, a child becomes so upset that he's no longer able to use his upstairs brain. Your toddler becomes so angry that you poured water on his head to wash his hair that he begins screaming, throwing toys out of the tub, and wildly swinging his fists, trying to hit you. In this case, the lower parts of his brain-in particular his amygdala-take over and hijack his upstairs brain.*

Children are natural scientists carrying out research and want to know the rules. Once they begin to understand that a temper tantrum is not the way to get the parents' attention at home, or to get something they want, they will want to know if the same rules apply in a variety of situations outside the home. We must be alert to this intelligent research and be clear.

Since prevention is always better than the cure, it is also helpful to learn about the needs of children so we recognize when they are not being met. Toys do not stave off boredom for long, but including a child in the daily life of the family — the work, the conversations, the laughter — beginning in the early years and sharing the work more and more as the child grows up, is a good beginning.

Busy parents just don't often have time to sit down immediately in such a situation, or the experience to analyze what is going wrong with a child. But perhaps an understanding of the two kinds of temper tantrums will help with this.

One of the ways of avoiding frustrations in children is to observe how many times we use orders instead of statements or suggestions. If a parent uses the same tone of voice for an important order as for a casual, not so important order, a young child will not be able to tell the difference. When children hear "no" or "don't" many times during a day, they tune us out because there is no way to know when the command is important ("Don't run out into the street.") or not so important or maybe impossible ("Don't ask me that question again.")

Here is an example from our home. A friend had brought her two-year-old for a visit. We sat down to the table to have orange slices for a snack. After a while the child got up from the table, picked up an orange slice and headed for the piano. The mother said, "Kino, don't take your orange to the piano." Kino looked back at her, paused, and then took another step toward the piano, looking toward his mother as though waiting for her to say something. She looked at me and said, "He used to be so reasonable and now he is doing things like this all of the time! What can I do?"

I replied, "I think he is doing research and wants you to tell him what the rules are. He is not being bad, he just wants to know."

She understood immediately, laughed, gently picked him up, and lovingly explained that, "Food belongs at the table, not the piano." Moving him physically from the piano to the table where we were eating made the message doubly clear for Kino.

We could almost feel his relief in figuring out just what his mother meant.

Montessori teachers try not to use directives, or direct orders, except in rare cases because one loses authority when directives are not obeyed; then a child becomes insecure, not knowing what the limits are. Instead of saying, "Don't talk so loud." say, "It is suddenly very loud in here." Instead of saying, "Put your coat on." say, "When we are both ready we can go." Instead of "Don't ask me that question again," one could say, "I see my answer wasn't very clear." This takes practice but it is very worth it.

### What about Good Behavior and Helping Children Feel Valuable?

For the child under the age of six years the best thing we can do is to be on our own best behavior as much as we can. Modeling behavior, and language, for a child can bring out the best in adults because we get to practice the ethics that we believe in.

When we can manage to take the time to include these young children in as many of our activities as possible during the day or week that can also go a long way to make them feel included and important. The resulting calm and happiness shows that ethical behavior, or goodness, whether secular or connected with a religion, is natural when the conditions are right.

One of the characteristics of a child older than six is an interest in good and bad behavior; children at this age want to try out the behavior they see out in the community; they enjoy long discussions about ethics and morality and religion. But we can share our religion, as well as our ethical behavior, with younger children by modeling and with practical life activities.

There is a history of Montessori being used to teach young children these things because the method of education aligns with the values and practices of a wide variety of formal religions and philosophies.

Here are some examples. Some I have experienced personally and friends and colleagues have reported others to me.

### Christianity

Montessori was raised a Roman Catholic. In 1990, during my Montessori 0-3 training, my husband and son and I were fortunate to visit an "atrium" in Rome. Atrium is the name given to a place where the tenets of Catholicism, the main religion of Italy, are shared with children at different ages by means of Montessori principles.

Sofia Cavalletti and a former assistant to Maria Montessori, Gianna Gobbi, founded this system many years ago in Rome. It was an honor to spend time with both of these women, as well as with Silvana Montanaro, who was teaching a class with young adults while we observed the 3-6 and 6-12 class.

Sofia was an academic with a doctorate in Hebrew who became interested in the religious potential of children, when the child of a friend fascinated her by a strong desire to learn, with interest and insight. Like so many of us, she "followed the child." In thinking about how to meet the needs of young children to learn about Catholicism, she learned about the Montessori methods and approached Gianna Gobbi who had a deep understanding of child development. The elements of the religion were analyzed and materials created so children from age 3-6 would learn about the stories of the Bible through practical life activities and sensorial materials.

Older children learned through timelines of the Bible very much like those that are found in Montessori 6-12 classes.

Above age 12, there were debates and conversations as profound as those by adults. Since then I have visited Montessori Atriums in Quito, Ecuador and in Bogota, Colombia.

One year while consulting with a Montessori school in Cusco, Peru I noticed that there was an altar in every classroom but each was on a shelf high up on the wall, at the adult's eye level. I explained what I had seen in Rome and Asia when children could participate. Later the head of the school told me that the altars were now at the children's height and both teachers and children are able to kneel on a soft pillows and pray at any time during the day.

As I write a book I often send chapters off to people I have worked with around the world because all feedback is valuable if I want to present the universality of children, and how Montessori principles work for all. Here is feedback from a Montessori 3-6 teacher who read this chapter when it was in progress:

*I always have in my classes an icon of The Virgin Mary. One day a girl came to tell me that she had something in her hand. When I asked her what she had she whispered to me, slowly opening her fist, "A rosary to put with Virgin Mary."*

*I was muted as I had never talked to the children about prayers or my faith, or why I had brought a Virgin Mary icon into our class. As the rosary was a silver one I asked her from where she had it, and she told me she took it from home without asking her parent's permission. So we decided together that it would be better first to talk to her mom and dad, and if they agree she can bring it back. The next day she came in very happy to me telling she had parents' permission so she placed the rosary on The Virgin Mary.*

*This opened the door to many conversations the children had about their religion, baptism, even sharing their family prayers before meals, and so much more. I thought to myself that I must nurture this interest and I know that your book is already helping me. Thank you.*

## Buddhism

While working in Asia I found that in almost every classroom, in Thailand and the Tibetan communities in India, there was an altar. This is a place where flowers are placed, incense is burned, and traditionally bowls are filled with water as one sends wishes for happiness for all out into the universe. Having something like this to care for and traditions to carry out focuses the children to think about caring for others.

In our home we have a family altar that the grandchildren look forward to at each visit. In the morning the steps are these: fill the pitcher with water, light the candle, from the candle light the incense and put it in the incense holder, then extinguish the candle flame with the candle snuffer. Then, one at a time, fill each of the traditional seven brass bowls with water.

After filling a bowl you can hold it in your hands, close your eyes, and (at age 3-6) think about what you are grateful for, or who you want to send good wishes to. An older child, because of a natural budding interest in social justice, usually would send good wishes to a situation that they decided needed help. Examples were, "I want to be nicer." "I hope the _____ river stops getting polluted." "I hope all of the cats and dogs at the animal rescue center find a home."

At the end of the day, the water is poured back into the pitcher and the now special water shared out among the houseplants, or garden plants. Then the bowls are dried and made ready for tomorrow.

Our grandchildren love this so much that we often, take turns filling the water bowls and sending out good wishes in the morning so everyone gets a chance each morning. We have sometimes had to work out a schedule, who does what morning and evening, to be sure that the steps are shared equally!

On our altar, inspired by the Mexican *Ofrenda* (altar) remembering those who have died, there are pictures of family members who are remembered as we pray. Also there are little statues, the collection having grown over the years, of animals, people, and even a little plastic Yoda to represent beings that might be living in other parts of the universe. The children understand that a sentient being means a being that has feelings. This can be a human or an animal, sometimes a tree or forest, maybe even a mountain or a river as is believed in some cultures. The grandchildren decided long ago that there is no way of knowing for sure just who or what has feelings.

In earlier times, and some places today, children participated in the work of the family from a very young age. They must have felt a valuable member of a family. But in our modern culture today there are sometimes very few possibilities for a young child to give to others. They are so well taken care of for the most part, fed and clothed and educated, the work of the family or society done by adults. Taking a moment to show gratitude or to pray, or in our case to think of seven beings or situations who might benefit from our sending good wishes to them is a simple and healthy way for children to feel useful and compassionate.

### Judaism

A favorite practical life exercise in a Jewish Montessori preschool is pouring grape juice into a special cup, braiding the Challah bread and baking it, and then saying the prayers for this special snack at any time during the work period. There are both Hebrew and English sandpaper letters, movable alphabets, and there are even Jewish Montessori organizations that help anyone wanting to share and introduce Judaism to children in enjoyable and meaningful ways appropriate for the stage of development.

In our family the grandchildren also have a Jewish grandparents so the Jewish celebrations, especially the lighting of the menorah at Hanukkah, have always been very special family events, privately at home or whenever we are all together.

## Islam

The co-director of school in Malaysia wrote to me:

*I've been interested in the work of Sofia Cavalletti and Gianna Gobbi for quite a long time. I find the connections between Montessori and all religions fascinating and it reinforces how Montessori education is truly universal.*

*Through their work I have discovered how Montessori and Islam also align so perfectly, especially in the philosophy of respecting the child and believing in the boundless potential within each child. Each of our environments has a small mosque, which contains a beautiful prayer carpet, the Quran, prayer beads and prayer clothing. The area is cozy and inviting. The children can come to this little mosque anytime during the work cycle and choose to sit, pray or read the Quran. The teachers also model and will sit in it for meditation or to read prayers. So for the child from 3-6 the connection with Islam is made sensorially through the environment and the adults. It is beautiful to watch.*

## Respect for Several Religions in a Classroom

In a Montessori school in the USA, I saw a little table that had objects from several different religions — a picture of Mary and Jesus, a little statue of Buddha, a Jewish Menorah, a candle and a vase of flowers, and a large beautiful shell to represent the creatures of the world. It was in a quiet part of the room with a chair inviting one to spend time looking at, caring for, becoming familiar with the symbols of goodness of the world. What a good way to be introduced to these ideas during the very young sensorial stage of life.

Many religions, maybe all, are concerned with helping human beings be honest, kind, generous, and caring of others. Some believe that children are born sinful and have to be directed to the right way. But Montessori has revealed to us the wonderful fact that we might all be born good and with great potential.

### *The Correct Kind of Work Heals*

When I am asked to explain Montessori "in a nutshell," I quote a sentence heard often in the Montessori world, "Work is the Normalizer." I explain that one of the most important skills of a parent or teacher is being able to match activities to the interest and stages of development of children. Then I explain the value of protecting ensuing concentration until children demonstrate that the work is finished according to their satisfaction. Here Montessori says it so well:

> *I observed . . . many more times. When the children had completed an absorbing bit of work,*

*they appeared rested and deeply pleased. It almost
seemed as if a road had opened up within their souls
that led to all their latent powers, revealing the better
part of themselves. They exhibited a great affability
to everyone, put themselves out to help others and
seemed full of good will.*

*It was clear to me that the concept of order and
the development of character, of the intellectual and
emotional life, must derive from this veiled source.
Thereafter, I set out to find experimental objects that
would make this concentration possible, and
carefully worked out an environment that would
present the most favorable external conditions for
this concentration. And that is how my method
began.*

*— The Child in the Family*

Maybe discovering and experiencing meaningful
and uninterrupted work, at any age, can help anyone
become a better human being: wise and compassionate,
hardworking, joyful, fulfilled and contributing members
of the family and social or professional group.

# Montessori at Home, Age 6-18

## Limits and Rules

Just as in the first six years of life, older children and adults need to understand the limits of behavior and the rules of various social groups. The last chapter explains clearly how to help set limits effectively in the first six years of life, and the same principles apply now. Here is an example with an older child.

I was staying with a friend in Russia who was frustrated because her son, age seven, was not obeying her. One day I observed him climbing up on a kitchen chair, and counter, to get some sweets that his mother had told him not to eat. I don't intentionally look for problems when I am visiting a friend, but my friend had asked for my help with this situation. My suggestion was for her to count, for one day, the number of times she said "no" or "don't". It was an enormous number! My friend cut down the number of orders in a day and her son started listening to and obeying her; her limits and rules were making sense to him.

## Giving

Also, children and young adults from age seven to eighteen on really need to be involved with real work of the family or the group in order to feel valuable, this is true from age six to eighteen, and for the rest of one's life.

We all need to have experiences of "giving back."

### *Letters, Cards, and Thank-You Notes*

It is wonderful when we have time to make personal holiday gifts for family and friends but life seems too busy these days to always do this. But writing Thank-you notes is an excellent way for children to give back. A personal detailed Thank-you note can be a precious gift from a child.

Every year at Christmas someone in the family has the assignment of writing down the gifts received by each person and who sent it – because our family is spread out all over the country, sometimes the world. Next, usually a day or so later, we gather to write thank-you notes. I have saved all of the thank-you notes sent from children and grandchildren over the years and love to look at them. The energy around writing them as a group is not something that one "has to do" but it is a group "giving."

In this picture you can see our family gathered in the living room here in California to write beautiful, detailed, decorated birthday cards for our mother/grandmother/great-grandmother who lived in Florida.

Such compassionate social, ethical, and religious values are at least as important in a child's education as reaching academic goals in when preparing for happy, successful lives. In Montessori the academic and the ethical curricula at this age cannot be separated.

### Ancient Wisdom

I have discovered through work in other countries that there is often an understanding that there are different needs and roles of human beings at different stages of life. This awareness is valuable in preserving the best traditions in a family, a community, and a society, both in the home and at school.

For example there is a saying in the Mongolian tradition that made me look at, from a new perspective, the methods we use to discover, and meet, the constantly changing needs of the human being throughout the stages of life. Here is a translation:

*A child should be treated as a God at 0-3; as a respected elder at 3-5; As a servant at 6-12, and as a friend from 13 years on*

### Age 0-3

This means that, just as we have learned about the child from birth to three years, the inner drive is very, very strong for good reason, and rather than trying to adapt this child to our needs we should use the best efforts to understand the needs of this age because this child is still considered "close to God."

### Age 3-6

We know that this child, just as in the early years, is watching, listening, learning, absorbing, and we must do our best to be respectful just as we would be to elders because this child is going to "do as we do, not as we say." A child actively respected at this age will, without effort, show respect to others throughout life.

### Age 6-12

The word "servant" in referring to the child from age 6-12 in this saying does not mean to be subservient to others, but to work! The child at this age is at the front line in chores, learning to carry out much of the household work, to function as a valuable and contributing member of the family, this first social group.

*Age 13-18*

Finally, from age 13 and onward, in treating this person as a "friend" means as an "equal", as this really is the first stage of adulthood. At this age both parties listen to each other's thoughts, respect each other's wishes, and engage in adult discussions about interests and life.

In many cultures, throughout history, many people have observed and supported the different needs at different ages.

### Cosmic Education – Understand Interconnectedness

During the preschool years children in Montessori environments and in many homes learn about all of the cultural areas—physics, botany, zoology, history, geography, art, and music—through their senses, experiments, pictures, models, and exploring the inside and outside environment.

In the following years, beginning at age seven, this basis invokes an interest in all of these subjects and how they interact with each other, nothing existing independently without connection of everything—we call the bringing together all of the areas of knowledge at this age Cosmic Education.

### A Cosmic Task - Finding One's Place in the World

Around age twelve we help children begin to think about how one could find a role, now and in the future, where one's own needs are met and at the same time one is contributing to the whole. This is known as a Cosmic Task.

Beginning at age 6-12 there is a great interest in society, of being an active part of a group, to make decisions as a group as well as an individual. It is a steady and strong time of life for academic and practical learning, but a lot of the need has to do with learning to live harmoniously with others. This creates a need to be a contributing member of a group. When all that education can offer is academics, this need cannot be met. It is no longer viable for casual apprenticeships in our country because of laws made to protect children, so we have to think hard to create these opportunities.

There is a DVD called *Ancient Futures* that has for years been used in Montessori classes for older children as part of the economic geography or environmental studies research. It tells the story of what happened when an ancient, balanced society in Ladakh comes face to face with the modern world in India. It compares globalization with localization, the value of which many people are talking about today. By the end there are many ideas on how to participate in creating a more balanced, local, community. After watching the video a 12-year-old Montessori student realized that she could have a part, at home, learning about and preserving the wisdom of caring for each other and protecting the environment. Her words:

> *Kids our age usually think there is nothing we can do to be helpful but this video gives us a lot of ideas and since in the future the world is ours we might as well start now. If we think about it no one can be truly happy when there is a lot of suffering in the world. Many people hear about all the suffering*

*that is going on but we think there is nothing we can
do so we just push that information aside. But
somewhere inside there is a little voice that tells me
that the suffering of others prevents me from being
truly happy myself. Now I understand that there are
things I can do to help and I don't have to hide the
truth from myself. I can listen to that voice inside
and do what I can every day to help, then I can be
truly happy.*

### Montessori Homeschooling

In our family we tried to follow Montessori
principles through the lives of our children, and now
grandchildren. There is some information about
homeschooling in the chapter of this book about the
Eureka, California newspaper column. The youngest of
our three children homeschooled — he educated himself
independently and reached out to others — through the
elementary, middle school, and high school years.

During these years, while also in graduate school, I
researched homeschooling in the United States and
discovered that there are many, many reasons for
homeschooling, and just as many methods of
homeschooling.

### Reasons for Homeschooling

Some parents want to protect their children from a
philosophy that goes against their religion or secular
ethics. Some parents want to spend more time passing
on their own wisdom or philosophy, or their own
passions and skills, to their children. Some parents want

a more personal teacher-to-student ratio for learning and cannot afford private schools or tutors. Some families live so far removed from any school that they have no choice but to homeschool aided remotely by teachers in another part of the country.

### Methods of Homeschooling

Some homeschoolers are required to sit at desks all day and raise their hands when they want to get up to go to the bathroom. Some homeschooling children are free to do nothing all day but play. Some families purchase materials or how-to homeschooling manuals, or they sign up for online schooling. Some homeschoolers stick to the curriculum dictated by the local educational department. Some do not.

### Our Own Homeschooling Experience

For our part we followed Montessori principles of including our son in the daily life and daily work as both parents worked full time, I in a home office. We watched carefully for his changing interests then guided him to research and create in that direction. We also kept the TV in a closet and got it out once a week for a movie, and limited computer use for a typing tutor program. So screen time added up to about 3-4 hours a week at the most. Above all, whenever he developed an intense interest in something, or was inspired to spend hours working on something, we knew the importance of not interrupting this kind of concentration.

We did not use Montessori materials because I knew, from years of teaching children in Montessori classrooms, that such materials are interesting to a child because they are observed being used by other children, not just because of a lesson of an adult. Also the reason the Montessori materials are so well made and expensive is because they are intended to be used by many children each day and to last for many years. It takes a lot of Montessori teacher training to know how to use Montessori materials, but even though I had the training and experience I knew they were not appropriate for the home. It was more valuable for us to make materials together because this was part of the learning process.

We sought out community activities such as soccer, art classes, music classes, swimming and even a group of like-minded families who started a "homeschooling school" where such children could gather for one or more days a week to play games, go on field trips, write stories and act in plays, and sometimes study math and geometry. We took our son along on business travel and took advantage of being able to explore these new cities with him.

Very importantly we were all constantly on the lookout for ways to serve others, such as feeding the homeless, playing music at senior centers, and cooking lunch once a week for an elderly neighbor. It clearly has become a way of life for all of us. During a gap semester during his university years we received this letter from Chennai, India:

> *Dear Mom and Dad, This morning two friends and I went to the Mother Teresa Orphanage and spent a couple of hours with the people there. All the kids there are ones that no one will adopt because they have some kind of physical or mental defect. A*

*lot of the kids had polio and couldn't walk, and one little girl was only about one foot tall and had a very deformed face. She had no arms either, only hands growing out of her sides. We spend a lot of time with her because I think that no one really plays with her because of all her imperfections.*

*There was a boy who had very weak legs so we spent awhile moving his legs for him and trying to get him to exercise them. Eventually he began to straighten and bend at the knees. He got very happy and started laughing when I touched his feet and moved his toes.*

*None of the women who ran the place spoke English, and the kids were completely mute except for one or two. We didn't really know what was wrong with some of the kids and we couldn't ask because we could not communicate with anyone, but we managed to help with some things. We went upstairs to a room where there were a bunch of sick boys lying down because they had measles and other diseases.*

*In a way I feel that this has opened up for me what is important in life and what is not so important. And I know that this feeling might not be with me for very long, but hopefully each time it sinks in a little deeper and stays with me longer.*

It was rewarding for us parents to see that our emphasis on the value of providing service during the homeschooling years had borne fruit.

Here is an excerpt from the end of the book about our own homeschooling experience, *Montessori Homeschooling, One Family's Story*. I think it applies to the work we are all doing, parents, teachers, and young people from age twelve to eighteen years of age and beyond.

> *When we understand human needs and tendencies at different stages of development, prepare an environment that calls forth the best work, and then get out of the way, nature can do the work of creating the complete human being. All the best that the human can be is already within all of us. All of us, and our children, have the potential to be happy, capable, confident, empathetic, hardworking, persistent, and kind human beings with an eye to understanding ourselves, to helping others, and to tackle the problems of the world, which are legion, all of this done in a spirit of joy.*

# A Montessori Grandparenting Story – *Eloise in Portland*

In the first three or four years of life a child is intensely interested in learning how the world works so we focus on giving this child the real world in all of the areas of the child's environment. We hold off on make-believe fairy tales and stories with talking animals until later. Reality in all its detail is fascinating to a child at this age.

Around age four or five however most children begin to understand that there is a difference between reality and make-believe. Their own stories (these are not *lies!*) reflect this exploration. The author Kay Thompson and illustrator Hilary Knight created books about a young girl known as Eloise that capture a child's attention during this transition. *Eloise in Paris* was one of our granddaughter's favorite books.

Here is what can happen when a child is given an opportunity to live out her literary fantasy. Zahra Sherman, age four (pictured on the cover of this book) experienced an "Eloise Party" with *Lala* (Aunt Ursula) and *Amala* and *Baba* (grandparents) at a Montessori conference hotel in Portland, Oregon. We had invited her because she loved the book "Eloise in Paris" about a little girl who lived in a hotel in Paris. We offered to recreate this story as closely as possible.

It was her choice whether or not to come with us; she was ready to risk it for only one night because Ursula, her aunt and full-time nanny, came with her. With our help Zahra, kept a journal that was later published in a Montessori magazine.

Each year the AMI Montessori teacher trainer and good friend, Joen Bettman, shared it during the language studies in her 3-6 teacher training courses. Here are her words:

*Dear Susan, The way that I have used this amazing Eloise story is to talk about prerequisites for writing and the value of spoken language. This dictation shows how a family (your family) can show genuine interest in listening, engaging in dialogue, making connections, being in the moment, and following the child. The grace and courtesy of playing a game and what one says to the winner/loser is also stellar. The audience has appreciated again and again the capacity of the child, the feminism, the humor, the importance of experience.... So thank you many times over for sharing. Fondly, Joen*

# Zahra Begins Dictating to Amala

*This is from my journal. Amala took lots of pictures for me to make a book. I told her what to write so I could tell a large story.*

FRIDAY

*Tonight I packed my suitcase, said good-bye to my parents, and told them they could phone me on Lala's cell phone if they got lonely.*

*As soon as we got to the hotel and up the glass elevator to our room I unpacked my suitcase and Amala started reading me the book about Eloise who lived in a hotel. When we got to the part about the lobby and the potted plants we put our shoes back on and took the glass elevator back down stairs to investigate the lobby and look for potted plants. There were a lot. We also went to see the swimming pool but it was covered up so we asked why at the front desk. The hotel person told us that it is only uncovered and used for swimming in the summer. I'll come back.*

*When we came back to our room we went out on the balcony to see the moon. It was silver. Then we got our sleeping bags ready, Lala and I did, and I took a bath. I asked Amala if there was anything else special at the hotel and she got a backpack out of her suitcase that looks like a little horse. She got it for me in Texas and I get to keep it. I put my sweater in it.*

*Baba and Amala have a bed with a lot of pillows on it. There is one pillow on each with the word "sweet dreams" on it. I got to use one of those.*

*Baba read books to me while Amala and Lala got ready for bed and then we all chose our breakfasts for room service and hung the menu on the outside of the door and someone will pick it up at midnight. Amala said it would be a man bringing room service because men are stronger than women. She just wanted to make Lala yell at her so she said that joke.*

*Both Eloise and I live on the top floor of the hotel. Eloise is make-believe, but it is still fun to have an Eloise party.*

SATURDAY

*Lala and I woke up very early but we whispered for a long time so Amala and Baba could keep sleeping. I told Lala that I wished it were still the first day because I really like to unpack my suitcase.*

*Finally the room service person brought us breakfast. It was a woman. We call breakfast petit dejeuner just like Eloise does. That is French. The petit dejeuner was wheeled into the room on a special cart covered with a tablecloth and cloth napkins and pretty silverware and china dishes. We had fresh fruit and juice, and milk and cereal and toast and jam and I don't remember what else. I was so excited that I didn't eat very much but I love room service. We ate in our pajamas. Amala wears a nightgown, but I never heard of anything like that before.*

*Now it is night and I am back at my hotel room. I decided to stay another night. Tonight Amala gave me another chess lesson and I learned about pawns and bishops and knights. They each have a special way to move and we played games. Baba read me a Simply Science™ book about spiders and another one about Eloise in Paris. We decided to visit the lobby again and saw a man playing the piano. I want to learn to play the piano because my mama knows how.*

*Today we took the glass elevator up and down a lot of times and could see the mountains and the hill where our house is. We are living on the 15th floor. Our room is 1559. I know how to find it and how to use the key to make the door open.*

*Before we went to bed we put lotion on our bodies and feet and hands and faces. It is hotel lotion and we get to keep it. At first it worried me that I would stay all gunky but then I kept rubbing it in and finally it was all rubbed in and my skin was soft. I get to take home the rest of the lotion.*

*Tonight Lala is sleeping in one of the beds and Amala is sleeping on the floor with me. She likes to read before she goes to sleep so I snuggle into my sleeping bag. Lala showed me how to do it so that my knees can stick out of the bottom to get air when they need to.*

*I think sleeping bags are more fun than beds. Well anyway, Amala read her book and told me I didn't have to go to sleep but that I should just read and try to keep my eyes open and I don't remember going to sleep but I did very soon. I like sleeping in a sleeping bag a lot.*

## SUNDAY

*This morning Baba went down to the conference early and phoned us to say that there were bagels and lots of fruit waiting for me so we got dressed and took the elevator down to eat with him at the conference. I watched a movie about Montessori schools, but I didn't know what high achievement is and I have heard the word* Montessori *but I didn't know what that meant either.*

*Amala told me that Montessori was a woman who changed schools. When I heard about what schools were like before I was glad that I get to go to a Montessori school. Children used to not have the freedom to walk around or talk or work with materials. I would not like that.*

*I got tired of watching movies so Amala and I took the elevator back to our room and played chess. Now I know how to move knights and pawns, and bishops, and rooks and the king and the queen. The queen goes on her color and can do just about anything she wants.*

*We packed our suitcases and I checked under the beds and in the drawers and in the closet and in the bathroom to see that we didn't leave anything. When I told Amala that I wish we could take the hotel chess set she told me that it didn't belong to the hotel, but that she and Baba had brought it for me. I am very excited about that. When I get home I am going to tell my parents all about chess, and that when a person loses he should say "I am very glad that you won and I enjoyed playing chess with you"*

*to the person who did win. Then that person should*
*say, "Thank you. I enjoyed playing with you too."*
*Sometimes we play games where no one wins. That*
*is good. Also I am going to see if I can have room*
*service at home, like Eloise.*

---

### Some time later:

About the time Zahra was writing her Eloise story in Portland, Oregon, a little boy was born in Kazakhstan. When he was 13 months old Dante was adopted and moved to the USA.

One evening a few years later Dante told his mother that he would like to write down everything about his life thus far, to be a kind of guidebook for children who might be going through a similar experience, but he felt that if he had to write it himself he would only get three words down and they would all be spelled wrong.

Earlier this same week his mother had read the "Eloise Story." Now she read it to him, and they were both inspired, she to act as scribe, and he to dictate his story to her. She wrote to me, "The floodgates of joyful tears opened and together we began…"

# Observation of a Montessori Class in London

Until this point I have focused on personal experiences of Montessori principles benefitting children and adults beyond the Montessori classroom.

To provide an example of how all of these same practices are followed throughout the day in an authentic Montessori primary, age 2.5-6, classroom I will share a personal class observation.

This was the children's class at the AMI (Association Montessori Internationale) teacher-training center in London where I had earned my first Montessori diploma in 1971. Now my oldest daughter was working toward her own diploma.

I was made welcome and invited into the class, even though this was the last day before vacation.

This brought back memories of observing other London classes during my own training, usually 30-40 children ages 2-7 with one non-teaching assistant.

I remembered one class in particular that had opened only two months earlier, where I sat down in the middle of the morning and had tea with the directress and watched the children. The class went on, a beehive of happy, calm, quiet activity, the children working independently, helping and teaching each other, and accomplishing an amazing amount of joyful work, uninterrupted by adult intervention.

This class was the same, exemplifying Montessori's words:

*What is the greatest sign of success for a teacher...? It is to be able to say, "The children are now working as if I did not exist."*

*— The Absorbent Mind*

One of Maria Montessori's most important contributions to our world was her discovery that humans have an inner guide which, if protected and nurtured in the child, can lead to the development of each person's full potential.

She gave us a practical method of providing a prepared and nurturing environment and setting the child free to flourish within it. A child who is in touch with this inner guide knows how and when and for how long to sleep, eat, move, talk, work, or think quietly. This child is enthusiastic, always happy.

To watch a prepared environment filled with 30-40 children functioning on this level, a "normalized class", is a thrilling experiences.

The following are notes from this observation on February 19, 1987:

### Class Composition:

Thirty children age 2 to 7 with one directress and one assistant.

To give an idea of what such a class can look like, here is a picture from another class in the UK taken later:

*Physical Environment:*

There is a small room that opens onto the main room. This is the "reception class" for under-twos, led by a 0-3 Montessori Directress (teacher) for two hours each afternoon, until the children feel ready to join the main group. This is a gradual process determined by the needs of each child. The main classroom is made of two rooms, one a few steps higher than the other, made into one large room in the ground floor of the training center.

The upper area opens into the garden. In warm weather the class takes place both inside and outside. Today it is snowing! The floor is of polished wood, the only carpeted area being the small reading corner that also contains a rocking chair and a few pillows.

The lower area, next to the reception class, contains fifteen tables, a nature corner, a book corner, practical life tables and shelves, math, language, a drying rack for paintings, physics experiments, and a shelf of toys similar to those in the reception class, for new children.

The upper area contains a snack table, piano, sensorial material, geography, history, music, globes and maps, a stack of floor mats, and a box of rolled larger floor mats. A corner shelf holds the record keeping charts readily available to the teacher throughout the day.

There is no directress' table, shelf, or desk. There is no storage area or adult-only material in the room.

There is an "ellipse" made of tape on the floor of the higher room for walking-on-the-line. Individual children use it throughout the day just as any other child-chosen activity. This provides practice in careful walking, sometimes by carefully carrying objects. As there are no compulsory large group or collective lessons held during the day, as sometimes is seen in Montessori classes, it is not used for sitting upon, for musical movement, or anything else but walking.

### The Schedule:

8:30 – The teachers/directresses/assistant arrive and prepare the environment.

8:45 - Children begin arriving, one adult keeping an eye on the coatroom (entrance hall) as children change from coats and outdoor shoes to indoor shoes (adults wear indoor shoes too) which are kept in colorful cloth bags hung on each child's coat hook. The adults' attention is completely on the children.

The children enter the classroom, greet their teachers, shake hands, and start the day as they wish, working or helping prepare the environment.

9:10 – The door is locked. Late arrivals must ring the bell and wait for the door to be opened. This helps the parents get the children to school on time, which is very important for the sense of order of all of the children.

9:30 - Activities in progress: mirror polishing, braiding, four cylinder blocks done blindfolded, silver polishing, number rods, drawing, puzzle map of Africa, classified picture naming (two groups containing two or three children, each led by a child), identical picture matching, decimal system introduction, pegboard (from toy, link-with-the-home materials shelf for new children), binomial cube, pouring rice, metal insets, and geometric cabinet with third set of cards.

10:10 - "False fatigue," a common occurrence early in the school year, or in a new class, occurs right on time. After about an hour of relatively easy work, the class is experiencing a period of restlessness as the children look about for the "great work of the morning" after which most children will settle down to concentrate well for an hour or more, emerging quite refreshed.

Rather than interfering, the directress steps back to wait for the class to settle back down. After a few weeks, as more children find longer and longer tasks to concentrate upon, false fatigue will not be seen.

Today the children have divided themselves into two groups, the younger children working in the lower room and the older in the upper room. False fatigue is

214

occurring only in the upper room. The momentary noise attracts the attention of the younger children who look up from their work for a moment, then go back to work.

10:50 - The assistant is leading a charming game with a few children, singing, choosing partners, dancing and bowing. Other children are continuing their work, unaffected by this circle game. A few children are helping the directress set up three tables, which will hold the hot lunch, which is being prepared in the kitchen.

In England the noon meal is the main meal of the day, even at home, and the children eat together.

### *Lunch Preparation*:

Two colorful, quilted hot plate mats are placed on a table, with a large spoon for soup. One child wheels the food in on a cart from the kitchen, then two other children, who have offered to help, set out stacks of soup bowls, a large tureen of soup, stacks of lunch plates, a plate of buttered bread, a plate of cheese slices, and a bowl of greens.

The directress and a child are checking the order and cleanliness of the rest of the classroom. It has been kept very ordered and clean throughout the morning by the children and the adults, so this is a quick task.

11:55 - The assistant is asking a small group of children if they would like to hear a story or a tape – the rest of the class is still working. They make their choice by voting and listen to a tape. A few children are signing a birthday card with the directress (for the cook).

There is a feeling of being in a home, a "children's house" rather than a school where children wait for an adult to tell them what to do next. The self-respect of the children is noticeable on their faces and in every action.

*Lunch*:

12:00 - After more than three hours of individual chosen work the children have quietly been invited, or have come on their own, and are seated at tables that have been moved, by the children, to create a collective eating area.

The directress stands and they all say a prayer together. Because there are no large collective or group lessons during the work periods this is the only time during the whole day that the children and adults are acting collectively, everyone doing the same thing at the same time with an adult leading.

I would like to stress this fact in order to encourage teachers who struggle to manage transitions of a group of children from one activity to another, often having to deal with children becoming bored and undisciplined in the process of waiting for the next activity:

THIS GROUP PRAYER BEFORE LUNCH IS THE ONLY TIME IN THE WHOLE DAY THAT CHILDREN AND ADULTS ARE ACTING COLLECTIVELY.

To begin lunch, the directress quietly calls three or four children at a time to begin serving themselves. The two teachers then sit down at one of the tables and eat with the children. For the next hour the serving, eating, talking, cleaning up, serving dessert, cleaning and dressing to go home (for those few children who go

216

home after lunch) is carried out solely by the children, while the directresses eat and talk with the children sitting nearest.

It is obvious that every detail of each of the lunch activities has been thought out, and taught to the children, with practical life lessons.

There is no feeling of confusion, tension, or control by adults and the children exhibit, even during lunch, the traits of normalized children—joy, dignity, independence, unselfishness, initiative, self-discipline, love of order, work, the environment, and each other.

Some of the practical life activities that are noticeable are: walking without bumping anything, tucking in chairs, holding chairs for another child, carrying a bowl of soup down two steps to a table on the lower level of the classroom, offering the last piece of food to another, checking to see if the bowls are empty before stacking them, looking in a mirror to see if one's face is clean, and not interrupting someone else who is talking.

During lunch the children are free to get up from the table, get more food, offer food to others, go to the bathroom, take as much food as they like (as at the snack table during the day). Again this is the feeling of a home.

After the main course, each child has cleared his place leaving his or her placemat on the table for dessert. A child pushes the cart back to the kitchen and the dessert is brought out. Again the children set out stacks of small bowls and spoons and two large bowls of pudding and berries. The rest of the class is talking among themselves at their tables.

Again the directress calls a few children to begin the serving, then sits down to chat while the children eat, converse, and clean up.

12:40 — As they finish, those children who are going home (5-6 very young new children) take a chair to a spot near the dressing area. Then each gets gets his or her outside shoes, boots, etc., dresses, and sits on his chair to talk to friends. The parents wait till the directress opens the door at 1:00. The children shake hands, say good-bye, and go home.

The rest of the class is still cleaning up, washing tables, putting chairs on tables for sweeping the floor, returned to their work, or are sitting and talking.

1:00 - Except for rainy days, the children who want to, go outside and play. The others stay inside and work.

1:30 - Children continue with work that is ongoing.

There is no feeling that the afternoon is any different than the morning. The children seem to need no special projects or adult-centered activities — even though this is the last day before vacation! Child-chosen work, by oneself or with one's friends, seems to be the most favorite activity of the children. The directress could easily say, "The children are now working as if I did not exist."

2:00 - The children are well into their work. The class seems the same size even though some have gone home because the children from the infant community that opens on to this room have come in and some are now working in this room.

Activities which I can see in progress right now are: sensorial square of Pythagoras (a 3-year old doing it very well), binomial cube, Africa puzzle map, thermic bottles, one child walking on the line, sandpaper letters and numbers, movable alphabet, polishing a classroom window, and table washing.

A child is able at any time to rest or sleep if he wants to. The directress tells me that children over 1 ½ seldom take naps in England (except for the convenience of the adult of course as in many schools) but tend to go to sleep earlier in the evening than American children.

The children are allowed to find their own balance between activity and rest.

The directress is working with a few children on a decimal system game. The assistant is going over the work records and observations. As in the morning children are free to work alone or with another, but only after asking if they can join another, because children learn to respect and not interrupt someone who is concentrating.

There is a rule "One can only work with a piece of material whose purpose she understands" but the "understanding" can come in different ways. She might have had a presentation one-to-one by the directress, by another child, or perhaps by watching another child's lesson or work. So the directress keeps track not just of the presentations she has made, but of all activities the child masters.

2:50 - The directress leaves the room for a parent conference. The children are working. As one child begins to walk on the line, the assistant helps him put on soft music and goes back to her work. Two other children join and walk on the line, balancing objects in their hands while they walk, and then they return to their previous work.

3:10 - The assistant sits down with a book near the door. This seems to be a signal to the children that the day is coming to an end. The children, for the most part, do not seem in a hurry to stop working. Over the next fifteen minutes they finish their work, put it away (or, were it not the last day of the term, neaten it to leave out for the next day), go into the hall and prepare for going home, dressing by themselves and helping each other. As they are ready they come and sit with the assistant and listen to her read.

3:30 - The outside door is opened. The children shake hands with the directress, say good-bye, and meet with their parents outside to go home.

The directress' attention, at the beginning and end of the day is on the children, not talking to parents.

### Errors and Their Corrections:

This is an established, normalized class, but I do not mean to give the impression that every action and intent was perfect! There were errors to be corrected. The beautiful thing is the method of their correction.

I watched the directresses carefully watching a child in each case to judge the intention. Then, unless it was something that needed to be interrupted at once (I saw this happen only once), a mental or written note was made so that the error could be corrected by teaching the correct activity later at a "neutral moment", rather than risk invalidating or embarrassing the child by reminding or correcting. "Teach by teaching not by correcting."

### Record Keeping:

A few Montessori directresses have told me that they reached a point in their careers where they thought they could "do it on automatic," without keeping detailed records of the children's lessons and mastery of work. Then they realized that their classes were no longer normalized and teaching was a lot more work! One of the important tools is definitely record keeping.

The directress of this class keeps these records:

**1. A daily record of the suggested presentations and the work of each child** — recorded during the day by the teacher, written on paper with a pencil in front of the children *very important modeling of writing*, then transferred to charts later, for each area of work.

**2. A running history of each child** — Recording the general adjustment and progress, twice a term (four times a year) or whenever anything significant occurs. This is very subjective so it is important that the various adults who deal with the child take turns making these notes. They are valuable for written reports and parent conferences.

**3. Concentrations Graphs or Work Curves** — Done for at least a couple of the children each week, or one a day. "We receive enormous help from the resulting graphs and follow up." — Directress

221

**4. Forecasts for each term** — These include a number of topics from each of the cultural areas relevant to the time of year, interests of the children, and so forth.

**5. Summaries within each area for each term** — A check for the teacher, to compare the forecasts in each area with what was actually done.

**6. Weekly plan** — This is based on what is, or is not, happening in the class in these areas: Math, Language, Sensorial, Basic Training, Practical Life, small group lessons, songs, games, finger plays, and all cultural areas (art, music, history, geography, physics, botany, and zoology). This is laid out in such a way as to allow a space for comments at the end of the week next to each item. "A valuable tool for self-evaluation."

These days in many places the adult: child ratio is usually dictated by an education department, and it is thought that the fewer children per adult the better. This is true in traditional setting when the adult does the teaching. But in a Montessori situation the adult puts the students in touch with the environment, and the children teach themselves.

*Note:*

When teaching at home it is very helpful for children to see the adults involved with, and interested in, their own work so the children can become independent and responsible.

# Stages of Development

*I have found that in . . . development, the child
passes through certain phases, each of which has its
own particular needs. The characteristics of each are
so different that the passages from one phase to the
other have been described by certain psychologists as
'rebirths'.*

— Montessori, *Four Planes of Education*

It has often been believed, at least in the last 100 years or so, that there is one standard body of knowledge that humans need to learn in order to be considered well-educated, one basic list of subjects to be mastered. And that the teacher should be in charge of imparting this knowledge in the same way, no matter the age of the child or adult.

However, many years of following Montessori principles has taught us that there are other skills that can be fostered in schools and homes that are more important, such as curiosity, exploration, work, concentration, creativity, patience, responsibility, and compassion.

We know that the way human beings learn these things differs widely according to the age and stage of development, or plane of development. Learning works best when these are considered and supported.

I am quoting liberally from Dr. Montessori's books in this chapter in hopes that the reader will be inspired to read them; they are as pertinent today as when they were written so many years ago.

> *The child's development follows a path of successive stages of independence, and our knowledge of this must guide us in our behavior towards* [the child]. *We have to help the child to act, will, and think for himself. This is the art of serving the spirit.*
> — Montessori, *The Absorbent Mind*

The following is a brief description of each stage. This information has proven helpful to parents of children of all ages, as well as both traditional and Montessori teachers.

### The First Plane, Age 0-6

Children naturally love and care about those things they know. So even by age six, when we give them experience with the real world, for example learning about the needs of plants and animals, they can develop a profound care for them.

At this age children love learning about the food, clothing, transportation, and housing of people in different cultures and different environments — mountains, seashore, deserts, jungles, and so on. They can explore, and learn to love, the physical sciences through simple experiments and by using their bodies to carry heavy objects, by feeling the rain, and watching the clouds. And they can learn how to take care of themselves, and each other. It is clear that even this young age is potentially rich in possibilities of learning about loving, and being a contributing member of the family and community.

> *During this period the personality undergoes great changes. We have only to compare the newborn babe with the six year old to see this.*
> — Montessori, *The Absorbent Mind*

> *There is in the child a special kind of sensitivity which leads* [the child] *to absorb everything . . . and it is this work of observing and absorbing that alone enables* [the child] *to adapt to life. The first period of the child's life is one of adaptation.*
> — Montessori, *The Absorbent Mind*

This is the motor-sensorial stage where humans learn by exploring through senses and through movement; this kind of exploration is the work of the child and when we observe deep concentration on this work we try not to interrupt concentration. The child learns self-control in an environment that meets these needs.

During the first three of the six years, from the first day of life, a child needs to be free to move, to explore the environment visually and then by touching. We can turn our attention to the environment at this stage.

Are there too many toys or materials available at one time? Is it clear where they can go when one is finished with them? Are the objects the child needs within easy reach in order to support independence of choice?

The child is watching carefully and learning. How do people treat each other? What do their words mean?

They watch how people move through space while walking, dancing, carrying objects, and so on.

Everything the family does, and their attitudes toward themselves and others are being observed; they will be imitated and become part of the child.

Chaos in the environment can cause stress, in children as well as adults. The need for order is inborn in the human being, but different for each person. In the Montessori class children are not "required" to put their work away, but they are taught how by challenges of carrying and placing objects, and the adult models the practice of putting materials away after they are used.

The second three years is similar, but children can now be given greater challenges such as learning about the world both in the family and outside in the community.

*Learning about the world*: The world of arts and sciences at this age is learned by exposure to, and chances to care for plants and animals, by seeing great art pictures, playing with water and carrying heavy objects, listening to stories by the parents, from books, music, everything in the environment.

*Practical life*: This work, including grace and courtesy, care of self, each other, and the environment, are often easier to do at home than at school. Parents can look for the beginning stages of any family activity and include the child gradually more and more. For example a child can learn to fold laundry, then put laundry away, then hand wash or help to use a clothes washer. This is the most important area of mastery in any Montessori class at this age for many reasons.

Executive function of the brain (planning, patience, self-control, attaining chosen goals, following logical steps, reasoning, problem solving) is improved during practical life activities more than in anything else at this stage, and can lay a solid foundation for all later learning.

*The senses*: At this age the senses are becoming more refined. Parents can provide experiences of, and give the language for, such concepts as *loud* and *soft*, *hot* and *cold*, *rough* and *smooth*, primary colors (red, yellow and blue), secondary colors (orange, green, purple), shades of colors, *dark* and *light*, a variety of tastes and smells, and eventually even comparatives and superlatives such as *large, larger* and *largest*, and so on.

*Language*: Receptive language begins before birth. Expressive language in the form of singing and speaking is gradual throughout this stage. Expressive language in the form of reading and writing preparation and mastery is also gradual.

To support learning to read and write, again it is the role of the parent to model the habit, and enjoyment of, reading books, and using a pencil to write. How can we expect children to do either if they are not exposed to these in the family? We should include the young child in our conversations with others, listen carefully to what is said by everyone, not just the adults, and avoid speaking about the child as though the child were not present in the room.

This is still the motor-sensorial period, so reading and writing preparation is aided by preparing the hand through fine motor activities such as pouring, digging in the garden, even playing with Legos. If a child shows an interest in letters we avoid capital letters and the names of letters and stay with lower case letters and the sounds these letters make. This prevents confusion and prepares the child in a logical way for both reading and writing.

*Math*: in the Montessori class at this age math is offered through materials experienced with the senses. Counting "one, two, three" is nothing but a poem, but if the child places objects carefully, one at a time — spoons placed in the dishwasher, Brussels sprouts placed in the cooking pot, blocks building a tower — counting each object "one, two, three" as each is placed, this is learning to count.

Fractions can be casually introduced by sharing food, "half for you and half for me" or, "Let's divide this banana into three parts and call each one a third. "I get one third, you get one third, and your sister gets one third." Examples can be found all around us and are the best way to awaken curiosity and introduce math as something enjoyable to learn about.

These activities are best introduced casually, not thought of as formal education with the child sitting down, paying attention, and memorizing. They should be offered and not required. We never know what will inspire a child to want to know more. We never know ahead of time what activity will inspire a child to work and concentrate for long periods of time. These experiences and concepts, as well as what a child observes in others in the family, will be a major part of the self-construction of the human being by age six. You will be amazed at what there is to explore in the home environment that can be experienced, named, and learned together with your child.

### The Second Plane, Age 6-12

> The next period goes from six to twelve. It is a period of growth unaccompanied by other changes. The child is calm and happy. Mentally, [the child] is in a state of health, strength and assured stability.
> — Montessori, *The Absorbent Mind*

With this kind of foundation the child from age six to twelve is ready to experience social life and academics with confidence, curiosity, and the desire to work and figure things out. This child asks big questions and interests include: *What is fair? What is bad and good? Why was I born? How was the planet Earth created? What is gravity? Where did language begin? Why do I need to learn geometry? What was the first word? What are the constellations called and what do they look like in different cultures?* And on and on . . .

*Since it has been seen to be necessary to give so much to the child, let us give . . . a vision of the whole universe. The universe is an imposing reality, and an answer to all questions. We shall walk together on this path of life, for all things are a part of the universe, and are connected with each other to form one whole unity.*

— Montessori, *To Educate the Human Potential*

At this age there is a gradual transition from motor sensorial exploration to that of the imagination. The child doesn't just want to know that our math system is based on the number 10, but why we have a math system at all, where did it begin, and what use it is to us! This new mind can easily reach back into the past and then reach conclusions about what might be coming in the future. This mind begins to be able to conceive of the tiniest particles of matter as well as the infinity of space. We must not limit them to our own educational experience, but provide ways for these big questions to be researched and answered.

Along with exploring the world, now outside the home even more than inside, there will be an exploration in behavior. The child thinks, "How will this new kind of speaking and acting that has been observed on the street be handled if I try it out at home?"

The parents will have to be continually thinking about limit setting, but this time discussing logical conclusions, the reasons for specific rules and limits, logical consequences, with our child as they come about. Fairness and justice, among family as well as among friends is an important part of exploration, work, and self-construction at this age.

Academically, especially if the foundation has been laid in the first five years — including experience in biology, history, geography, arts, and sciences — academic curiosity will be ready to learn more. And even if this is not the case, a desire to learn about the world in these areas is still a driving force at this age.

The curriculum in the 6-12 class is based on five areas. Each one is an introduction to the formal studies that will follow through out all education. These are: the creation of the universe (physical sciences), the timeline of life (life sciences), timelines of humans and civilizations (studies having to do with humans), language (the history and development and mastery of languages), math and geometry (the history, variety, function, and reasons to study these subjects.).

In class all children are introduced to all of this work, but NOT as subjects to be mastered and graded as a group as in traditional systems. A minimum of work in each area is required, and then each student marks out an individual path through these six years, depending on interests. This is delightful to see.

In working some children want to work with others in a group or have music playing as they study, but some children, just as some adults, need privacy and silence to concentrate. We are all aware of our own needs as far as an environment that supports deep concentration, and our own working and learning styles. Now we must observe to see the needs, and work styles for individual children. As Dr. Montessori says in the above quote, age six to twelve is a relatively calm period of life, a time where a great deal of learning can be accomplished if the social and educational methods meet the needs of this child for self-guided exploration, self-imposed work, and activities that meet the self-construction need for physical, mental, and social growth and responsibility,

### The Third Plane, Age 12-18

Beyond age twelve, we have before us young adults. When they are treated as equals these people will rise to their potential. They are ready to learn about greater responsibility, earning and budgeting and spending money, finding ways to help others, and fulfilling more challenging roles in the family or society.

> *The adolescent must never be treated as a child, for that is a stage of life that he* [or she] *has surpassed. It is better to treat an adolescent as if he had greater value than he actually shows than as if he had less and let him feel that his merits and self-respect are disregarded.*
> — Montessori, *From Childhood to Adolescence*

This third plane is very much like the first, especially age 0-3, in many ways:

— There is rapid physical growth, brain growth and pruning (elimination of brain cells that have not been used)

— There are changes in the personality with a push-pull relationship with the adults as the child fulfills the strong need to act independently.

— Because of the rapid growth there is a constant change in how others respond to one, sometimes causing confusing and potentially affecting the young person's self-image.

— There is a need to tap into one's intuition as far as food and sleep.

— There is a need for a lot of processing or thinking time as one figures out where to put all of these new experiences and feelings during the process of self-construction.

> *The third period goes from twelve to eighteen,*
> *and it is a period of so much change as to remind one*
> *of the first. There are physical changes also during*
> *this period, the body reaching its full maturity.*
> — Montessori, *The Absorbent Mind*

The needs and methods of education for the adolescent are so different from anything so far available in the world of education that there is now an AMI (Association Montessori Internationale) diploma for teaching at this stage, called *The Adolescent Orientation*.

I believe that the most useful Montessori book regarding this age is, *From Childhood to Adolescence*. I also have written a lot about this age in *Montessori Homeschooling, One Family's Story*.

### The Fourth Plane, Age 18-24

Ancient civilizations often have provided a clear role for this, the fourth plane of development, and also for the third plane, as a young person became an adult.

But in today's world there is an extended need for academic or professionals studies that takes up all of the young person's time and energy. When these requirements are the main concern, with no understanding of the needs according to Montessori philosophy, serious problems can, and do, arise. We see this happening all over the world.

> *Education should therefore include the two*
> *forms of work, manual and intellectual, for the same*
> *person, and thus make it understood by practical*
> *experience that these two kinds complete each other*
> *and are equally essential to a civilized existence.*
> — Montessori, *From Childhood to Adolescence*

An understanding of the needs of these years has been a major focus of my cultural research and I hope that some of the earlier chapters in this book will be helpful for parents and teachers searching for a balance.

### Adults

We adults also go through stages of development. It has been my experience that the more a parent or teacher learns from observing and living with children and young people, the more chance we have to understand ourselves, and to meet our own changing needs, as we grow and develop in our understanding and experience of life.

Through many years of experience in Montessori schools and in homes that support Montessori ideas, it has been shown that human beings have an amazing potential to be happy and compassionate, to work hard and continue to learn throughout life, and to contribute to society.

We now have several generations of people who have grown up being supported in the ways presented in this chapter. I have met many of them and they are formidable in their passion to have meaningful lives, and desire to help the world be a better place.

I think Montessori would have been very pleased with the result of her work and inspiration.

*My vision of the future is no longer of people taking exams and proceeding from secondary school to University but of passing from one stage of independence to a higher, by means of their own activity and effort of will.*
    — Montessori, *From Childhood to Adolescence*

h

# Conclusion

Following Montessori principles can help anyone dig deep and discover inborn gifts. A child nurtured in this way, as a complete human being, will have the experience and confidence to push boundaries, to fail without fear of judgment, and to think in unique ways. We are living in an explosion of creativity and the world needs human beings who excel in creative problem solving, resilience, and compassion.

*Times have changed, and science has made great progress, and so has our work; but our principles have only been confirmed, and along with them our conviction that mankind can hope for a solution to its problems, among which the most urgent are those of peace and unity, only by turning its attention and energies to the discovery of the child and to the development of the great potentialities of the human personality in the course of its formation.*
*— Montessori, The Discovery of the Child*

# Resources and Books

### Educateurs sans Frontières, montessori-esf.org

EsF is a network of Montessori practitioners, working with communities, organizations and other partners to advance human development from the prenatal stage to early childhood care and education, continuing through to elementary, adolescence, adulthood and the elderly.

### The Aid to Life Initiative, aidtolife.org

This helpful site was created with several Montessori groups working together. My daughter Ursula helped with the text and I filmed several of the video clips. It focuses on the first three years of life, presenting development in the areas of movement, communication, independence, and self-discipline.

### Montessori for Dementia and Aging, montessoridementia.org

This program shares Montessori wisdom that improves the lives of elders, promoting the principles of dignity, meaningful engagement, and independence throughout life.

### The Montessori Adolescent Initiative, montessoriadolescent.org

The goal of this initiative is to conduct a study of the developmental needs of humans during the age 12-18, and to train adults to create ideal environments in which to work with and teach young adults

### Montessori Sports, montessori-sports.com

This is an AMI Montessori certified course that provides one with the basic knowledge on how to integrate child-centered, rather than the typical adult-centered sports into Montessori environments across all planes of development, preschools through high school and also to integrate Montessori principles into regular sports environments.

### The International Montessori Index, montessori.edu

This site was begun in 1998 to alert the general public that the name *Montessori* has no legal protection and can be used by anyone for any purpose. Here are suggestions as to what to look for in a search for a Montessori school or teacher training center. It was created in collaboration with AMIUSA (The Association Montessori Internationale of the United States, NAMTA (North American Montessori Teachers Association), Loyola University of Baltimore, and Susan Stephenson.

### Montessori Model United Nations (MMUN) montessori-mun.org

In collaboration with the United Nations, this program for international Montessori students from 9-15 years of age, gives valuable experience at the stage of life when young adults are interested in reason, justice, and morality.

### Shree Mangal Dvip (SMD) Boarding School, himalayanchildren.org

The SMD School serves the needs of children who come from some of the most vulnerable places, the northern villages of the Nepal Himalayas.

### Kanthari, www.kanthari.org

Kanthari is the project in Kerala, India begun by the co-founders of Braille Without Borders (BWB) after the school for the blind in Tibet was closed.

### Susan Mayclin Stephenson Home Page, susanart.net

Up-to-date work by the author of this book

## *The Joyful Child: Montessori, Global Wisdom for Birth to Three*

This is an overview of the Montessori birth to three Assistants to Infancy program begun in Italy in 1947. It was finalized in coordination with Silvana Montanaro, MD, AMI trainer, who wrote the introduction. It shares, with both parents and teachers, clear and simple text, illustrated by many pictures, that help support emotional, physical, and intellectual growth at this age. A chapter on child-centered weaning, and a comparison of Montessori 0-3 practices and traditional 0-3 practices in the country of Bhutan are included.

*The Joyful Child* has been used as a text in Montessori adolescent human development courses, birth preparation classes, and university education classes. It is recommended for Montessori 0-3, 3-6, 6-13 teacher training courses. It has been translated into thirteen languages.

*Susan Stephenson's book truly reflects the spirit and purpose of Montessori in a way that makes the philosophy translatable to both new parents and veteran Montessorians. Susan's passion for the pedagogy, her extensive experience, and her world travels resonate as she explores the universal, emotional, and psychological depths that construct the child's development.*
— Virginia McHugh, Past Executive Director of The Association Montessori International USA

*This is a very accessible and beautifully illustrated introduction to Montessori infant years. I believe every new parent should read this book and pass it along to family members, friends and caregivers. I can't praise it highly enough!*

— Rochelle Foles, Family Coach, Poet, USA

# Child of the World: Montessori, Global Education for Age 3-12+

An overview of Montessori philosophy and practice for parents and other educators. *Chapters Include*: **Age 3-6:** Caring for Oneself, for Others, and for the Environment; The Preparation and Serving of Food; Toys and Games; The Earth, Physical Sciences; Plants and Animals, Life Sciences; People, Social Sciences; Music and Art; Language; Geometry, Math, and Measurement. **Age 6-12**: Transition to the Elementary Years; The Earth, Physical Sciences; Biology, Life Sciences; The Humanities, Social Sciences; The Arts; Language; Invention, Geometry, and Math. **Age 0-24**: Stages of Development; The Young Adult Age 12-18; The Adult, Age 18-24

*I have a greater understanding of Montessori education from reading Child of the World than I have gotten from my various other readings about Montessori practice and philosophy. Thank you for centering Montessori principles on the needs of children and families.*

— Patrick Farenga, Editor of the homeschooling newsletter *Growing Without Schooling*

*This book explains the meaning of life, how you are supposed to live it. It would be helpful to other people my age. If the young person does not want to read the chapter, The Young Adult, Age 12-18, then the parents should read it so they can help their son or daughter become a better person.*
— Ryan Alcock, Age 13, Amsterdam

*Stephenson's volume is a wonderful resource for parents seeking thoughtful, sound advice on raising well-grounded children in a chaotic world. Presenting Montessori principles in clear and eloquent prose, Stephenson's legacy will be a tremendous service to generations of parents to come.*
— Angeline Lillard, PhD, Professor of Psychology, University of Virginia, author of *Montessori, The Science behind the Genius*

# The Red Corolla, Montessori Cosmic Education (for age 3-6+)

Based on the author's lectures during the first Montessori 3-6 course given in Casablanca, Morocco. This book, describing the first work in the Montessori 3-6 class, provides a solid foundational experience that prepares one to participate fully, as an older student and as an adult, in environmental and social justice.

*Chapters include*:

*The Work of the Adult*—creating an album that fills in the gaps in the teacher's general knowledge

*The 3-6 Children's Culture Album*—practical life, sensorial, and language lessons, in the areas of physics, botany, zoology, history, geography, music, and art

*The Leaf Collection, and Botany Classification Outline*—including detailed lessons exploring botany

*Formal Language/Poetry Album*—Directions for creating a language album to be added to year after year

*Two articles* previously published in Montessori journals: *The Child's Discovery of a Global Vision and a Cosmic Task*, and *The Music Environment from the Beginning to the End*

*What I like about this book is the possibility that it will give to teachers who have not learned in their training this way of presenting the various cultural areas – art, music, geography, biology and physics – to young children. That is, how to offer it in such a way that the child freely chooses to absorb the materials. Scattered throughout the book is information on approaching various ages of children, not just the young one.*

— Rita Zener, PhD, AMI 3-6 Montessori Teacher Trainer

*Thank you for the richness of information you brought. I have never seen such an extended cultural area offered to students on Montessori courses before and I think this is indeed a great gift to them. It was a great gift for me, also, even if I am just a translator and not a Montessori trained person, yet.*

— Miruna Molodet, French translator for the first AMI 3-6 course in Casablanca

*I love all of your books and "The Red Corolla" is no exception. Whenever I read one of your books I feel like I have both my mom and a teacher guiding me. Your writing style is therapeutic for me. This is a valuable resource for anyone who wants to deeply understand the Montessori approach.*

— Claudia Dumitrascu, Computer Scientist, Romania

## *The Universal Child, Guided by Nature*

This book is based on the presentation given at the 2013 International Montessori Congress in Portland, Oregon. Examples from around the world show that Montessori is based on meeting the human needs for exploration, movement, work, maximum effort, perfection, concentration, and self-control. These same needs are evident at all ages but show themselves in different ways depending on the age and stage of development from birth throughout childhood, and adulthood. There are details of the author's experience sharing Montessori throughout the world. (Age 0-18)

*Traveling with Susan Stephenson through this book was a pleasure. Montessori practices applied to all cultures today, highlighted by the author's experience in many countries, and the eloquent photographs, generated in me a great enthusiasm to continue my journey through this path. Thank you for being a source of inspiration.*

— Perla Aurora Britez Larrosa, Montessori Teacher, Paraguay

*Simple, elegant, inspiring. Susan Stephenson carries Dr. Montessori's vision of education for peace forward with this lovely, simple book about what we can all recognize as universal in our make-up as human beings. Those things that ought to (and can) bring us to a place of great respect for children through positive, intelligent engagement with them the world over.*

—Gioconda Bellonci, Montessori Teacher

## *Montessori and Mindfulness*

Based on the presentation at the AMI International Congress in Prague, Czech Republic in 2017, the main point of this book is simple. When we put the emphasis of protecting uninterrupted periods of self-chosen work, and concentration, rather than merely covering a specific academic curriculum, the result will be mindfulness, happiness, compassion, love of work, and more—for the adult as much as the students.

*Chapters include*: Mindfulness; Meditation as a Path to Mindfulness; Montessori and Mindfulness from the Beginning of Life; Mindfulness Support and Impediments (in the Montessori Environment); Flow, the Secret of Happiness; Work as Mindfulness, Mindful Walking; Music as Mindfulness; Mindful Exploration (including information and pictures on the Morocco orphanage "first year Montessori project"; Born to be Good; a chapter by Angeline Lillard, entitled "Mindfulness Practiced in Education: Montessori's Approach." (Age 3-18)

*The author has a deep and broad understanding of Montessori and life long experience with meditation. Supplemented by wonderful pictures and stories from worldwide travels, this book gives a sound portrayal of how mindfulness manifests in this most profound and wise approach to children's education. Many thanks!*

— Angeline Lillard, PhD, Professor of Psychology, University of Virginia, author of *Montessori, The Science behind the Genius*

*The author writes with such clarity and simplicity yet takes on the complexity of Montessori philosophy and contemporary thoughts on mindfulness with such grace and care. Her overall theme that personal fulfillment leads to care for others and for our environment echoes throughout each chapter and creates a wonderful symbiosis of Montessori thought and Mindfulness practices, with interestingly retold personal stories throughout. I really like the way Susan distills the essence of Montessori into such an accessible and inspiring book.*

— Lynne Breitenstein-Aliberti, Association Montessori Internationale, United States

## *No Checkmate,*
## *Montessori Chess lessons for Age 3-90+*

In this book teaching chess is just one example of how a parent can analyze an activity in order to teach it in an enjoyable way according to the child's stage of development. *Chapters include*: Chess Grace and Courtesy; Three Levels of Learning Chess; Taking turns; Ending a Game; Helping Each Other; Advanced Chess moves and rules; Cooperative or Non-competitive Board Games; The Benefits of Chess

*If you are looking for a book that will help you to introduce the game of chess to your child — in a non-competitive, gradual, and fun way — you have found it! Deep respect and understanding of human development in its formative stages is a common denominator of all Ms. Stephenson's books. In*

No Checkmate *you will find a conceptual framework of developmental characteristics along with a practical guidance in form of preliminary games and activities, gradual introduction to the key rules of the game, and more. This book opened a new field of exploration and joy for me and my two daughters!*

— Dmitry Ostrovsky, Israel and Russia, Father, Philosopher, Montessori Teacher

## *Montessori Homeschooling, One Family's Story*

This book shares the highs and lows of twelve years of exploring not only academic learning, but also the meaning of life. Both parents worked full time, the mother in her home office, thus the student learned early how to keep records of work, manage time and complete self-assigned work. *Chapters include*: How We Began, The Grades, (then a chapter for each grade from Kindergarten through high school), Final Thoughts. (Age 6-18)

*We do not home school and we were not really familiar with Montessori until reading this book. Here I learned the importance of looking at the big picture of what education is all about. Most importantly it is about kids learning they are part of a family, community, society. It's about learning compassion for others, and being kind and respectful to all. I am a Grandmother whose grandchildren spend half the time with us. Now our grandkids have been able to feel valuable in helping with all of the daily work of the family. Also because of this book many of our dinnertime conversations include discussions of different cultures and academics of all kinds. This book validates the importance of learning outside of a traditional school setting; it brings to our awareness the fact that real education can help children uncover their own unique gifts. This book is a tool for parents and grandparents desiring to make all this possible for their kids.*

— Sherry Vanderpool, A California Grandmother

*The author shares valuable, informative methods for how to teach and interact with children and teens. I am using the author's techniques at work with children from ages 7-18, with great success. Susan shares ways to treat children with respect and dignity and receive that respect in return. Examples of how to achieve reciprocity are abundant in this gem of a book. This is a must-have for parents or people working with children of all ages and backgrounds.*

— Kathy Wollenberg, Counselor for Young Adults, USA

*This book is amazing – a must read for all parents and Montessori elementary teachers.*

— Joanne King, Parent and 3-12 Montessori Consultant, Netherlands

*Each chapter describes one year of home schooling from Kindergarten through twelfth grade and beyond. It is a virtual compendium of "how to do Montessori schooling" encyclopedic in detail and charmed with honesty about failures and successes. This is quite a span, with the right kind of limited stimulus exposed at the right ages and stages and leading to wider independence. It comes through with the widest scope at adolescence. They had four guidelines: keep the developmental stage in mind, prepare the environment and offer the work, observe to see if it is working, and lastly, adapt and "follow the child". This Montessori-inspired home-schooling centered in the family ended with Michael's acceptance at Brown University. It is more than a fairy tale; it is a triumph for all families to witness.*

—David Kahn, Director Emeritus of NAMTA, North American Montessori Teachers Association, and adolescent education speaker and consultant

# THE AUTHOR

Over the last fifty years Susan has carried out a variety of Montessori work in thirty-two countries on six continents. Her goal has always been to learn as much as she teaches, to understand Montessori through the eyes of the people she works with, and to be able to help others in as many ways as possible. This is her eighth book, each one expressing Montessori from a different perspective.

Susan is a parent and grandparent. She has AMI (Association Montessori Internationale) diplomas for 0-3, 3-6, and 6-12. She has a degree in philosophy from San Francisco State University, a master's degree in education from Loyola University in Baltimore, and she studied multiple intelligences under Howard Gardner at The Harvard Graduate School of Education.

She has worked as a counselor for adolescents, a Montessori school administrator, a guide for parents of infants and toddlers at home, and a teacher of children and young adults, from one to eighteen years in Montessori environments.

Susan has lectured at education conferences for many different organizations, and is a school consultant and an AMI (Association Montessori Internationale) oral examiner for teacher training courses. Susan has been invited by educational departments of national governments in such places as Thailand, Mongolia, Peru, Colombia, Russia, Sikkim, and Romania, to speak to teachers about using Montessori principles for their students.

She and her husband homeschooled their youngest child through elementary, middle, and high school. They live in Northern California, near the coast and surrounded by redwood trees.

Her website is www.susanart.net

Manufactured by Amazon.ca
Bolton, ON